THE PENGUIN CLASSICS

FOUNDER EDITOR (1944–64): E. V. RIEU

EDITOR:
Betty Radice

MARCUS AURELIUS ANTONINUS was born in A.D. 121, in the reign of the emperor Hadrian. At first he was called Marcus Annius Verus, but his well-born parents both died young and he was adopted, first by his grandfather, who had him educated by a number of excellent tutors, and then, when he was seventeen, by Aurelius Antoninus, his uncle by marriage, who had recently become emperor, and had no sons of his own. Aurelius Antoninus changed Marcus' name to his own and married him to his daughter, Faustina. She bore five children, but none of them survived except the worthless Commodus, who eventually succeeded Marcus as emperor.

On the death of Antoninus in 161, Marcus made Lucius Verus, another adopted son of his uncle, his colleague in government. There were thus two emperors ruling jointly for the first time in Roman history. The Empire then entered a period troubled by natural disasters, famine, plagues and floods, and by invasions of barbarians. In 167, two years before the death of Verus left him in sole command, Marcus went to join his legions on the Danube. Apart from a brief visit to Asia to crush the revolt of Avidius Cassius, whose followers he treated with clemency, Marcus stayed in the Danube region and consoled his somewhat melancholy life there by writing a series of reflections which he called simply *To Himself*. These are now known as his *Meditations*, and they reveal a mind of great humanity and natural humility, formed in the Stoic tradition, which has long been accepted and admired in Christian Europe. He died of an infectious disease in camp on March 17th 180 A.D.

MAXWELL STANIFORTH was educated at Charterhouse and Christ Church, Oxford, where he held a classical scholarship. Plans for an academic career were frustrated by the outbreak of war in 1914, and for the next four years he served as an infantry officer on the Western Front. After the war he became a railwayman on the British Railways in Argentina, eventually leaving with the rank of Assistant Traffic Manager. He returned to England to take Holy Orders and after twenty-five years as a parish priest retired as Rural Dean of Blandford in Dorset. Since then he has translated two works for the Penguin Classics: this present volume and *Early Christian Writings*.

MARCUS AURELIUS
MEDITATIONS

TRANSLATED
WITH AN INTRODUCTION BY
MAXWELL STANIFORTH

PENGUIN BOOKS

Penguin Books Ltd, Harmondsworth, Middlesex, England
Viking Penguin Inc., 40 West 23rd Street, New York, New York 10010, U.S.A.
Penguin Books Australia Ltd, Ringwood, Victoria, Australia
Penguin Books Canada Ltd, 2801 John Street, Markham, Ontario, Canada L3R 1B4
Penguin Books (N.Z.) Ltd, 182–190 Wairau Road, Auckland 10, New Zealand

—

This translation first published 1964
Reprinted 1966, 1967, 1969, 1970, 1972, 1974, 1975, 1976,
1977, 1979, 1980, 1981, 1982, 1983, 1984

—

Copyright © Maxwell Staniforth, 1964
All rights reserved

—

Made and printed in Great Britain by
Hazell Watson & Viney Limited,
Member of the BPCC Group,
Aylesbury, Bucks
Set in Linotype Granjon

CONTENTS

INTRODUCTION

A couple of generations ago *The Meditations of Marcus Aurelius* was very fashionable reading. That was the time when every good publisher's catalogue included an elegant series of miniature classics; and there were very few of these in which the *Meditations* failed to make its appearance. The vogue has passed away now, but it may explain why the book is still known by name to so many people, even though acquaintance with its contents is rarer than it once was. Indeed, when you pick up this volume, you may well ask yourself, 'What is it going to be about? What sort of stuff shall I find inside it?' Let me say at once, then, that you need not expect any continuous or connected theme. This is simply the private journal or 'commonplace book' in which Marcus Aurelius jotted down from time to time anything that struck him as worth preserving. At one moment he is recording a thought suggested by some recent event or personal encounter; at another, musing on the mysteries of human life or death; now he is recalling a practical maxim for self-improvement, now copying a quotation from the day's reading which has taken his fancy. All these, and a wide variety of other items, are set down just as they occurred to the writer. You may take up the book or lay it down at any point you choose, and read as many or as few of the entries as suits your mood. Marcus, in short, has provided us with an excellent book for the bedside.

The *Meditations* is customarily, and no doubt rightly, classified by librarians under the heading of 'Philosophy'; but this may give the reader a misleading impression, unless he understands the place which philosophy held in the ancient world. From what he knows of the writings of its twentieth-century exponents, he is unlikely to conclude that its chief aim and end is the attainment of personal virtue. This, he imagines, is the province of religion, not of philosophy. But in classical times things were different. Morality, the good life, man's relations with the gods – all these were the domain of the philosopher, not the priest. Roman religion in the Imperial age had no concern with moral problems. Its business was simply the performance of such appropriate rites as would ensure the gods' protection for the State, or avert the effects of their displeasure. It was a formal system of public ceremonies carried out by State officials, and provided no answers to the doubts and difficulties of human souls. Yet then, as now, men found themselves perplexed by the great questions that are the common concern of us all. What is the composition of this universe around us, and how did it come into being? Is it ordered by blind chance, or a wise Providence? If gods exist, do they interest themselves in mortal affairs? What is the nature of man, and his duty here, and his destiny hereafter? It was not the priests but the philosophers who claimed to supply the answers to such inquiries. Their answers, it is true, were not unanimous; there were rival systems of philosophy, and each proffered its own solutions (as, for that matter, the different world-religions of our own day still do); but all were agreed that the sole right to pronounce with authority in the fields of metaphysics, theology, and ethics belonged to philosophy. It was believed to be competent to unfold the story of creation, define the unseen powers behind the world-order, expound the nature and purpose of human existence, prescribe the rules for right living, and reveal the future that lay beyond the tomb. Thus philosophy took the place which in our day is occupied by religion, as the instructor and guide of souls at every stage of their earthly pilgrimage. Such a claim is especially justified in the case of Stoicism, which was marked by a more religious character than any other ancient system. As the historian Lecky observes, 'Stoicism became the religion of the educated classes. It furnished the principles of virtue, coloured the noblest literature of the time, and guided all the developments of moral enthusiasm.' *

What this amounts to is that a reader who wishes to approach the thought of Marcus Aurelius in the right way should remember that the emperor's frequent allusions to 'philosophy' always carry the kind of implications we associate nowadays with the word religion. For philosophy, to the man who wrote these *Meditations*, meant everything that a religion can mean. It was not a pursuit of abstract truths, it was a rule for living. In a sense, this book is as truly a manual of personal devotion as Thomas à Kempis's *Imitation of Christ* – with which it has often been compared, and which is indeed its Christian counterpart.

The Stoic Philosophy

Stoicism, the system of philosophy in which Marcus believed, was originally a product of Middle Eastern thought. It had been founded some three hundred years before Christ by Zeno, a native of Citium (now Larnaka) in Cyprus, and received its name from the 'Stoa', or colonnade, at Athens where he was accustomed to discourse. His chief disciple was Cleanthes, who in turn was followed by Chrysippus; and the successive labours of these three men, who were afterwards held in veneration as the 'founding fathers' of Stoicism, had resulted in the formation of a scheme of doctrine embracing 'all things divine and human'. The three keywords of Zeno's creed were Materialism, Monism, and Mutation. That is to

* *History of European Morals*, vol. i, p. 225.

say, he held that everything in the universe – even time, even thought – has some kind of bodily substance (materialism); that everything can ultimately be referred to a single unifying principle (monism); and that everything is perpetually in process of changing and becoming something different from what it was before (mutation). These three tenets were the bedrock on which Zeno built his whole structure. His uncompromising insistence upon them led him occasionally into propounding ideas that were clearly indefensible; but in the hands of his successors the more rigid assertions of the founder were modified and softened in such a way as to make them acceptable to thinkers of a more realistic turn of mind.

When Stoicism passed from the East to the West and was introduced to the Roman world, it assumed a different aspect. Here it was the moral elements in Zeno's teaching that attracted the chief notice, and their practical value was promptly appreciated. A code which was manly, rational, and temperate, a code which insisted on just and virtuous dealing, self-discipline, unflinching fortitude, and complete freedom from the storms of passion was admirably suited to the Roman character. Consequently the reputation and influence of Stoicism increased steadily all through the centuries which saw the decline of the republic and the rise of the principate; and by the time Marcus Aurelius ascended the throne it had reached the height of its supremacy. Its conceptions and its terminology were by now familiar to educated men and women in every important city of the Empire.

The Stoics defined philosophy as 'striving after wisdom'; and 'wisdom' in turn was defined as 'the knowledge of things divine and human'. They divided this knowledge into three branches: Logic, Physics, and Ethics.* Since the first requi-

* Cleanthes subdivided them into Logic and Rhetoric, Physics and Theology, Ethics and Politics.

site in the search for truth is clear and accurate thinking, which itself depends upon a precise use of words and a vocabulary of technical terms, the initial study was Logic. After that came the investigation of natural phenomena and the laws of nature. This extended up to the metaphysical interpretation of the universe; for in the Stoic scheme Physics included the complete study of Being in its threefold manifestation – man himself, the created universe around him, and God. Last of all, holding the highest and most important place in the system, came Ethics. For the real business of philosophy, the point towards which all other inquiries converged and to which all other branches of knowledge were subservient, was the proper conduct of man, defined in a word as 'virtue'. As Diogenes Laertius puts it, 'they compare philosophy with a living creature; its bones and sinews corresponding to Logic, its body of flesh to Ethics, and its soul to Physics. Or again, they liken it to a fruitful field, of which Logic is the surrounding fence, Ethics the crop it bears, and Physics the soil.' * It will be convenient to summarize briefly their teaching on these three subjects.

(a) *Logic.* In the department of Logic, all that the reader of Marcus Aurelius need be acquainted with is the Stoics' theory of knowledge and of the means by which it is attained. In their system knowledge begins with *impressions*, which are produced by the impact of things or qualities on the senses. It is then in the power of the mind to pass judgement on what the senses report: to *assent* to it as a truthful presentation of objective reality, or to reject it as false. (The critical importance of this step is stressed repeatedly by Marcus.) Some impressions, of course, will command immediate and spontaneous assent – for example, the elementary notion that good is beneficial and evil harmful – but in other cases assent is

* Diogenes Laertius, vii, 40.

given only after deliberate reflection; and it may vary from a hesitant approval, so weak and faltering as to constitute a mere 'opinion', up to the positive assurance that is produced only by a so-called 'arresting impression'. This is an impression so strong that, in the words of one writer, it 'seizes upon the subject, as it were, by the hair and extorts his assent'. Nevertheless, even an impression of this kind may in fact be imperfect or misleading; and consequently the assent founded upon it, no matter how assured, may be mistaken. It must therefore next be submitted to the scrutiny of reason, the sovereign power which alone can issue the passport to *conviction*. Finally, this personal conviction must be verified by comparison with the experience of past ages and sages, and confirmed by the general verdict of mankind; and it then becomes *knowledge*. In explaining these four stages, Zeno used to illustrate impressions by the outstretched fingers, assent by the closed hand, conviction by the clenched fist, and knowledge by the fist gripped tightly in the other hand.

(*b*) *Physics*. Stoic physicists taught that the primordial source of Being in all its forms is a certain substance, omnipresent in the universe, which can best be described as Mind. However, since they were thoroughgoing materialists, this Mind was held to consist of a real and positive stuff, though of the thinnest and most impalpable kind imaginable. Borrowing an analogy from the subtlest and most lively of known elements, and one which also nourishes life and growth, they conceived its essential nature to be that of Fire; but a Fire so rarefied and ethereal that the word 'heat' perhaps comes closer to describing it than anything which might suggest ideas of actual flame. This Mind-Fire, which possessed consciousness and purpose and will, was both the creator and the material of the universe; it took shape in innumerable different manifestations, so giving all things their particular substances and forms, and producing out of itself the visible world and all within it. According to the various contexts in which he is thinking of it, Marcus has many names for it: when he dwells on its operations upon the universe as a whole, he may call it God, Zeus, Nature, Providence, Fate, Necessity, or Law; as one of the material elements in nature, it is Fire, or Air, or Force; in relation to the constitution of man himself, it becomes Soul, Reason, Mind, Breath, or (in the technical language of Stoic psychology) 'the Master-Faculty'. It is important to remember that all these words are simply terms for the same creative Mind-Fire in its varying aspects.

Stoicism is thus a pantheistic creed: that is to say, it holds that God is immanent in all created things, but has no separate existence outside them. As such, it is in direct opposition to the rival teachings of Epicureanism. Epicurus, developing the ideas of Democritus, maintained that the only constituents of the universe are atoms and empty space. Atoms in infinite numbers are in continuous high-speed movement in the void, and their fortuitous collisions lead to certain combinations which make the world what it is at any given moment. Since this ceaseless clashing of atom with atom in the vortex is forever giving rise to new combinations and dispersions, the life of the universe continues to perpetuate itself inexhaustibly. It is true that among the infinitely numerous possible combinations some are bound to look as if they were the result of design; but in reality there is no such thing as design, and all is due to chance. Marcus himself, in more than one passage of the *Meditations*, considers the implications of this alternative theory. 'Is there a wise Providence, or only a jumble of atoms?' he asks; but it is only to conclude that in either case the moral issues with which he is concerned would be unaffected. For his own part, his conviction of the providential guidance of the world does not waver.

To explain the process of creation, the Stoics relied on the theory of *tension*. From the fact that most bodies expand when heated, it is clear that heat exerts pressure. Accordingly the Mind-Fire, in its primal state of intense heat and correspondingly high pressure, at once begins to expand; and this brings about a proportionate slackening of tension. As a result, some of the divine fire cools and becomes visible as the humbler element of earthly fire; this again, as the tension continues to weaken, partially condenses into air; and portions of the air, in turn, solidify into water and earth. At this stage a movement in the opposite direction sets in; the vital heat contained in these four elements begins to assert its creative energy, and to materialize in the countless shapes and forms which compose the universe. Physically, these are differentiated by the varying proportions of fire, air, earth, and water contained in them; in other respects, their nature depends upon the degree of tension in the generative fire. Thus at a certain grade this force will realize itself as the organic forms of vegetable life; at a higher degree, as the animals or 'souls without reason'; and after that, as the 'reasoning souls' distinctive of men. Within these categories as many different forms of being can be produced as there are differing degrees of tension. At the maximum tension, the Mind-Fire takes on the attributes of a World-Soul, holding the same relation to the universe as the individual soul to man himself. At long last, however, a time comes when this ever-mounting energy reaches a pitch of intensity at which it becomes the devourer of its own creation: one after another the different forms and substances dissolve back into their original elements, the water evaporates into air, the air turns to flames, and finally the universe disappears in a grand conflagration which leaves nothing surviving but the primordial Mind-Fire itself. There-upon the whole process straightway begins again; the successive acts of creation repeat themselves, and the pattern of history starts to unroll as before. All this recurs in endless cosmic cycles of alternate creation and destruction; and since the eternal laws are unchanging, after each conflagration every event that has happened in previous cycles must reproduce itself once again down to the smallest detail.

As for man himself, he is a microcosm reflecting faithfully in itself the vaster organism of the universe. His physical body is formed out of the four elements, and that which creates, indwells, and controls it is a particle of the omnipresent Mind-Fire. Just as this fiery Power at its highest and purest acts as the soul of the world, so here, residing in the body in a scarcely less ethereal form, it plays the same part for man, generating and directing his life, his senses, his thoughts, and his emotions. It is nourished by the blood, and has its seat in the heart, the chief centre of the blood. (Hence Marcus twice refers to the soul as 'an exhalation from the blood'.)

At the appointed time Nature disperses the material elements which have composed the body, in order to use them for other purposes; and this is what we know as death. As to what happens to the 'fiery particle', Stoics, like Christians, are not unanimous. All agreed that it must sooner or later be re-absorbed into the primal Mind-Fire, but there were differences of opinion as to when this took place. The earliest doctrine, to which Marcus adheres, was that after the dissolution of the body the soul lived on in the upper regions of the air, and was not resolved into the World-Fire until the final conflagration. This was the teaching of Cleanthes; Chrysippus, on the other hand, opined that it is only the souls of the good and wise which thus preserve their personal identity until the end of the world, the bad and unwise being allowed but a brief period of survival before their re-absorption. Other teachers held that in every case this re-absorption followed immediately on death; and others again believed in a purgatorial state in which the soul underwent physical and moral purification as a prelude to its reunion with the world-substance.

(c) *Ethics*. The Stoics taught that the chief end of man, and his highest good, is happiness. In their view happiness was attained by 'living according to Nature'. This celebrated phrase is too easily misunderstood by the modern reader. It does not mean living the simple life, or the life of the natural man; still less does it mean living just as one likes. To grasp its significance, we have to remember that 'Nature' is one of the Stoic names for the divine fire which, besides creating all things, also shapes them towards their proper ends. Thus it embodies the idea which we nowadays express by the term 'evolution': the American poet who wrote 'Some call it Evolution, and others call it God' came very near to the Stoic way of thinking. It was the force which guided and directed every kind of growth or development towards its ultimate perfection; and because it was also a force that was alive, purposeful, and intelligent, the Stoics themselves did in fact sometimes call it God. 'Live according to Nature', then, was a maxim not very different from the New Testament injunction, 'Be ye followers of God', and implied an equally lofty ideal and an equally arduous discipline.

If we ask for a more precise definition of this 'Natural Life', Marcus says that it consists for every creature in a strict conformity with the essential principle of that creature's constitution. In the case of man, this essential principle is his reason, which is a part of the universal Reason. In so far, therefore, as he follows this rational law of his being, he approaches happiness; in so far as he departs from it, he falls

short of happiness. The Natural Life, in fact, is the life con-
trolled by reason; and such a life is briefly described as
'virtue'. It is this meaning of virtue which explains the Stoic
dogma that 'virtue is the only good, and happiness consists
exclusively in virtue'.

Reason tells us plainly that some things are in our power
and others are not. For instance, bodily health, wealth,
friends, death, and such like are not ours to command; therefore they can be neither helps nor hindrances to the Natural
Life. They are 'things indifferent'. But our own will, our
judgements, our power to accept what is morally right and to
reject the contrary - all these are in our own power. It follows
that nothing external can by itself affect us; it is not until we
inwardly assent to it or refuse it that we can be harmed or
benefited. Pleasure by itself is not a good, nor pain by itself
an evil; they become so only if we judge them to be so. This
is the meaning of Marcus's insistence that 'opinion is everything'. It also explains the wise man's readiness, which we
find emphasized so often in his pages, to 'accept without resentment whatever may befall'; a precept which is clearly one
of the mainstays of his own personal life. This is the principle
behind the famous 'apathy', or passionlessness, of the ideal
Stoic sage. Such a one, the philosophers taught, will experience all the sensations and emotions which are the
common lot of man, but because he refuses to view them as
evils they will not perturb him. Regarding them as things
external and therefore indifferent, he remains secure and un-
harmed. Consequently, as the Stoics paradoxically asserted
(to the amusement of the Epicurean poet Horace), the wise
man alone is the true king, rich in spite of his poverty, happy
in spite of physical torments, free even if a slave, serene and
self-sufficing through all vicissitudes. Should circumstances
ever prove too much for this perfect detachment, he will not

hesitate to take a voluntary departure from life; for mere life by itself is also among the things that are indifferent. Both Zeno and Cleanthes died by their own hands, and we shall find Marcus himself more than once toying with the thought that in certain conditions it better becomes a philosopher to leave life than to remain in it.

As unequivocal as man's duty to himself is his duty to others. Since all men are manifestations of the one creative Mind-Fire, the doctrine of universal brotherhood played a leading part in the Stoic system. The rational and social instinct is something that is inherent in the constitution of man. Kindness to his fellow-creatures is therefore at all times incumbent upon him; he must school himself to be tolerant of their failings, make allowance for their ignorance, forgive their misdoings, and help them in their need. To Marcus this was not always the easiest of tasks; the very frequency with which he reminds himself that neighbourliness is an important part of the Natural Life suggests that in practice it was sometimes a strain on his powers of benevolence. Nevertheless, he recognizes to the full that man is a social being, made for social action. He accepts the Stoic axiom that the whole universe is an organized society; a civic community in which the divine and the human dwell together in a common citizenship. (Earlier, the Cynics had described it as the *cosmo-polis*: the city which is co-extensive with the whole cosmos.) In his own words, 'the world is as it were one city'; and just as to the Athenian Athens was the 'dear city of Cecrops', to the philosopher the universe is the 'dear city of God'.

Marcus Aurelius Antoninus

Marcus Annius Verus, the future ruler of Rome, was born on 26 April A.D. 121, in the reign of the emperor Hadrian. His father, Annius Verus, was a Roman nobleman; and his grandfather, of the same name, had been Prefect of the City and three times Consul. Both his parents died young, and on his father's death Marcus was adopted by his grandfather, of whom he writes with warm affection and respect. The years of his boyhood were happy and studious; a series of the ablest tutors cared for his education and trained him in the doctrines of the Stoic philosophy; and though his health was never robust he enjoyed riding, hunting, wrestling, and out-door games. When he was seventeen the emperor Hadrian died and was succeeded by Aurelius Antoninus (usually known as Antoninus Pius), whose wife was Marcus's aunt Faustina. Having no son of his own, Antoninus adopted his wife's young nephew, changed his name to Marcus Aurelius Antoninus, named him as his successor, and betrothed him to his daughter Faustina. How much happiness Marcus found in this marriage must remain an enigma. The contemporary chroniclers delight in retailing stories of her shameless profligacy, and declare that she was treated with culpable indulgence by a husband far too good for her. However, the evidence for this is doubtful; and it is certain that when she died, thirty years later, Marcus grieved for her loss. She had borne him five children, of whom he was passionately fond; but death robbed him successively of all of them except the worthless Commodus, who lived to succeed his father.

From his seventeenth to his fortieth year, as the close companion and colleague of Antoninus, Marcus was occupied in learning the arts of government and preparing himself for the future duties of empire. In those years the majestic immensity of the *pax romana*, maintained by the Imperial administration, stretched over the whole of western and southern Europe, north Africa, Asia Minor, Armenia, and Syria. But much of the burden of governing this vast dominion centred on the person of the emperor himself; and when Antoninus died in 161, a heavy weight of responsibility descended on Marcus. Against the wishes of the Senate, he took Lucius Verus, the other adopted son of Antoninus, as his colleague on the throne; and Rome was presented for the first time with the spectacle of two emperors. Almost simultaneously came the end of the long years of Imperial serenity. An outbreak of plague spread disastrously over the western world. Floods destroyed great quantities of grain at Rome, obliging Marcus to sell the royal jewellery to relieve his starving subjects. In addition to the anxieties of pestilence and famine he found himself harassed by the alarms of war. Peace was broken by the clash of arms; on the eastern frontiers fierce tribesmen of the Marcomanni ('men of the marches'), Quadi, and Sarmati poured over the border in a series of determined attempts to pierce the Empire's defences. Faced by this threat, Marcus left Rome in 167 to take command in person of his hard-pressed legions on the Danube. In 169 Verus died, and for most of the next thirteen years Marcus remained alone at the post of duty. For a brief interval he was called to Asia, where the commander of the troops, Avidius Cassius, revolted and caused himself to be proclaimed emperor. But Cassius was murdered by two of his officers; and it is characteristic of Marcus that when they brought the severed head to him he recoiled in disgust and refused to see them. He ordered all the papers of Cassius to be burnt unread, and treated the rebels with clemency. During this expedition to the East his wife Faustina, who had accompanied him, died; and Marcus returned to the Danube to resume his task of holding back the onrushing tide of barbarism. There, among the misty swamps and reedy islands of that melancholy region, he consoled the hours of loneliness and exile by penning the volume of his *Meditations*. Laborious years of toil and conflict had by now exhausted his spirit; he was weary of life, and in his own words 'waiting for the retreat to sound'. When at last an infectious disease attacked him in the camp, he lingered for a few days and died on 17 March 180, in the fifty-ninth year of his age and the nineteenth of his reign. 'Weep not for me,' were his last words; 'think rather of the pestilence and the deaths of so many others.'

To suggest that Marcus was not a true Stoic seems paradoxical. Nevertheless, his meditations indicate a type of character that would hardly have satisfied Zeno or Chrysippus. The varying moods of hope and depression, the sensitive shrinking from disagreeable associates and sights of blood, the repressed but evident longing for sympathy and affection – these are not the signs of a temper cast in the antique Stoic mould. The truth is that Marcus represents a transitional phase of thought. In place of the old assurance of self-sufficiency there is a diffidence and a readiness to acknowledge his own failures; instead of the Stoic virtue of pride he seems to anticipate the Christian virtue of humility. All the more, then, do we sympathize with his recurrent struggles for self-mastery, and his efforts to direct every natural impulse and emotion into the stern service of duty. No doubt this constant preoccupation with the perfecting of self, this reiteration of improving maxims and moral platitudes, has produced a distasteful impression on some readers; and there have even been detractors who have called Marcus a humbug and a prig. Such a judgement, I think, shows a failure to understand the nature of the religious temperament; for when a man takes his religion seriously, conscientious self-scrutiny and aspirations to virtue are bound to form a very large part of all his inward thoughts and meditations. After all, the writings of a St Paul or a Thomas à Kempis exhibit as many moral admonitions, exhortations to sanctify and citations of canonical

authorities we find in Marcus; yet no one has had the hardi-
hood to accuse their authors of insincerity – even despite their
avowed intention to write for the edification of a large circle
of readers. When, on the other hand, we overhear the philo-
sopher-emperor's secret communings with his own soul, and
remember that at no time is he addressing any human auditor
but himself, I believe every instinct tells us that we are in
the presence of a man who is simple, humble, and utterly
sincere.

One small but significant fact, which so far as I know has
not been noticed by any of his editors, seems to indicate his
genuine goodness of heart. When he has occasion to refer to
persons in terms of approval, he never fails to record their
names. But when, as sometimes happens, he allows himself a
comment that is unfavourable, a veil of secrecy is drawn over
the offender, and we are left with no more hint of his identity
than is furnished by an unrevealing 'he' or 'they'.* This
charitable habit – which might perhaps be commended to
some who write their memoirs in our own day – deserves
particular notice in one whose sensitivities must have suffered
almost daily affronts from the manners and society of the
period.

'Lead me, Zeus and Destiny,' says the prayer of Epictetus,
'whithersoever I am appointed to go. I will follow without
wavering; even though I turn coward and shrink, I shall
have to follow all the same.' The words fitly express Marcus's
attitude to life. If he remarks wryly that it is 'more like wrestling than dancing', his fortitude does not fail; and the peculiar
sweetness and delicacy of his character have an attraction that
is not lessened by this tincture of gentle pessimism. 'By nature
a saint and a sage, by profession a ruler and a warrior,' from
the lonely height on which he stands he contemplates the

* e.g. III, 15; IV, 6; IV, 28; VII, 52; XI, 14.

sorrows of mortality with eyes that are disillusioned yet serene. 'And so', to quote Matthew Arnold's tribute, 'he remains the especial friend and comforter of scrupulous and difficult yet pure-hearted and upward-striving souls, in those ages especially that walk by sight, not by faith, but yet have no open vision : he cannot give such souls, perhaps, all they yearn for, but he gives them much, and what he gives them they can receive.' And of his equestrian statue which stands in the Piazza Campidoglio in Rome Henry James has written that 'in the capital of Christendom, the portrait most suggestive of a Christian conscience is that of a pagan emperor'.

So long as men are attracted by the tears and triumphs of human goodness, Marcus Aurelius will not lack readers. Wistful, compassionate, and disenchanted, this last of the Stoics still puts our weakness to shame and our discontent to silence.

Stoicism and Christianity

In conclusion, the reader may usefully be reminded that the theology of the Christian Church owes a large debt to Stoicism. In the original gospel of Christ the moral and spiritual elements predominated, and the intellectual element was wholly subservient to them. But when the message spread beyond the confines of Palestine, and its implications were assimilated by thoughtful men in other lands, the need for more exact conceptions of the truth made itself felt. It became evident that the new faith must raise a multiplicity of questions in the fields of cosmogony, metaphysics, psychology, and ethics; and for all of these the Church had to discover some coherent system of answers. Fortunately, much of the material for the task lay ready to hand. The ground had already been explored by the schools of pagan philosophy, and their findings constituted the accepted body of contemporary scientific knowledge. Many of the men who flocked into the Christian community during the second century had been educated in these doctrines from their youth; the majority of them in the principles of Stoicism, since that system more than any other attracted the naturally religious type of mind. To them, therefore, the churchmen turned for aid in building the structure of their theology. This is not to imply an uncritical or wholesale appropriation of the pagan ideas. Rather, when a philosophical theory seemed to suggest the lines along which Christian thought might seek its own solution of a problem, it was taken as a working hypothesis and tested for its possibilities; after which, in a suitably modified form, it might find its place in the new religion. In the words of Dr Prestige, 'the idea was cut to fit the Christian faith, not the faith trimmed to square with the imported conception'.*

For example, the author of the Fourth Gospel declares that Christ is the *Logos*. This expression (meaning either 'reason' or 'word') had long been one of the leading terms of Stoicism, chosen originally for the purpose of explaining how deity came into relation with the universe. According to the philosophers, the divine Reason had brought the world into existence through the agency of innumerable particles of itself, which indwelt and gave form to every created thing. This version of the origin of the universe, already deeply impressed upon his contemporary generation, was accepted in principle by the evangelist. He asserts, however, that the medium through which God manifested himself in the creation and maintenance of the world is not a multiple but a single and personal *Logos*, begotten of himself. 'In the beginning was the Word, and the Word was with God, and the Word was God. All things were made by him, and without him was

* *God in Patristic Thought*, p. xiv.

not anything made that was made.' * Thus Christian baptism is given to Stoic metaphysic.

Another Stoic concept which furnished inspiration to the Church was that of 'divine Spirit'. Cleanthes, wishing to give a more explicit meaning to Zeno's 'creative fire', had been the first to hit upon the term *pneuma*, or 'spirit', to describe it. Like fire, this intelligent 'spirit' was imagined as a tenuous substance akin to a current of air or breath, but essentially possessing the quality of warmth; it was immanent in the universe as God, and in man as the soul and life-giving principle. Clearly it is not a long step from this to the 'Holy Spirit' of Christian theology, the 'Lord and Giver of life', visibly manifested as tongues of fire at Pentecost and ever since associated – in the Christian as in the Stoic mind – with the ideas of vital fire and beneficent warmth.

Again, in the doctrine of the Trinity, the ecclesiastical conception of Father, Word, and Spirit finds its germ in the different Stoic names for the Divine Unity. Thus Seneca, writing of the supreme Power which shapes the universe, states, 'This Power we sometimes call the All-ruling God, sometimes the incorporeal Wisdom, sometimes the holy Spirit, sometimes Destiny.' The Church had only to reject the last of these terms to arrive at its own acceptable definition of the Divine Nature; while the further assertion that 'these three are One', which the modern mind finds paradoxical, was no more than commonplace to those familiar with Stoic notions.

Other instances of Christian ideas which had previously been taught by the Stoics are the conviction that men are 'God's offspring'† and partake of his nature, and the consequent belief that we should regard all men as our

* John i:1.

† Quoted by St Paul (Acts xvii:28) from the Hymn of Cleanthes.

brothers and neglect no opportunity of benefitting a fellow-creature. One of the later New Testament writers has also stamped with Christian authority the Stoic belief in the final conflagration of the universe.* A notable Stoic contribution, too, to the manners of the Church, and one which has had a lasting influence, was the practice of asceticism. Christians who desired to follow counsels of perfection took the Stoic sage and his way of life as their formal exemplar. The coarse garment, the untrimmed locks and beard, were adopted as the badges of aspiration to sanctity. Just as the Stoic professor was accustomed to withdraw from society and meditate in solitude, his Christian imitators not only followed his example but appropriated his terminology. In the Stoic vocabulary one who went into retreat was an 'anchorite'; one who practised self-discipline was an 'ascetic', those who lived apart from their fellows were 'monachi', and the place of their retreat was a 'monasterium'. Each of these borrowed expressions has retained its place and significance in the language of the Church to this day.

Perhaps the best evidence, however, of the way in which Stoic ideas penetrated Christian thought is found in a treatise which became the basis of medieval moral philosophy, the *Duties* of St Ambrose of Milan. Here the scriptural conceptions of righteousness and holiness are almost wholly displaced by the former doctrines of Stoic orthodoxy. The voice is the voice of a Christian bishop, but the precepts are those of Zeno. Not godliness, but happiness appears as the ideal of life; and the happy life is a life according to nature. Such a life is achieved by virtue, for virtue is 'the highest good'; and virtue is once more resolved into its ancient pagan elements of justice, prudence, temperance, and fortitude. Most remarkable of all, the happy and virtuous life is declared to be fully

* II Peter iii : 7, 10.

realizable during our sojourn here on earth; and the hope of future bliss becomes not a primary but only a subordinate motive.

In the face of these and similar pronouncements by a prelate and doctor of the Church, who will deny the right of Stoicism to be called, in the words of a writer of our own age, 'a root of Christianity'?

THE HYMN OF CLEANTHES

HIGH GLORY OF THE COMPANY OF HEAVEN,
LORD OF THE MANIFOLD NAME,
ETERNAL AND EVERLASTING IS THY POWER!

BLESSED BE THOU,
O GREAT ARCHITECT OF CREATION,
ORDERING ALL THINGS IN THE WAYS OF THY LAWS!

TO CALL UPON THY NAME
IS MEET AND RIGHT FOR MORTAL KIND,
FOR WE ARE BORN OF THYSELF;
YEA, AND TO US, TO US ALONE
OF ALL THAT LIVES AND MOVES UPON THE EARTH,
IS GRANTED A VOICE AND AN UTTERANCE.

THEREFORE NOW WILL I SING PRAISES UNTO THEE!
THEREFORE NOW AND FOR EVER GLORIFY THY POWER!

TRANSLATOR'S NOTE

It must be admitted that this work begins straight away with a mistranslation. The Greek title at the head of Marcus's book does not mean 'Meditations' at all; the meaning of its two words is simply 'To Himself'. I do not know who was first responsible for paraphrasing them as 'Meditations', but long usage has now accustomed the reading public to this name in preference to any other, and so it seemed pedantic to discard it in the interests of a more literal accuracy.

The earliest English translations of Marcus Aurelius were made by Meric Casaubon (1634) and Jeremy Collier (1701). Casaubon's style, besides being archaic, is cumbrous and involved; Collier's rendering strays so far from the original that it is scarcely more than a paraphrase. Neither work can be said to have had great popular success. The first man to bring a wide public under the spell of Marcus Aurelius was the nineteenth-century scholar George Long. His translation was published in 1862; it is admirably correct, as literal as a school crib, and to me at least utterly unreadable. Nevertheless, it quickly became a cultural 'must' to the mid-Victorian generation, from great and eminent persons like the Dean of Canterbury and Matthew Arnold down to innumerable lesser folk; and during the next forty years the number of its printings and reprintings in different styles and sizes must have been legion. Perhaps this is not wholly surprising, for it does not need much imagination to picture Marcus himself as the very figure of an admired Victorian personage; the grave dignity, the improving sentiments, the earnest piety of the *Meditations* were in the fullest accord with the taste of that era.

In 1898 there appeared a translation which many critics have since pronounced to be the most lively, scholarly, and idiomatic of all English versions, and I like to remember that this was the work of my old headmaster G. H. Rendall. (Since Marcus teaches us to remember with gratitude the instructors of our youth, it is a pious duty to record here my debt to Gerald Rendall, who first introduced us at school to the *Meditations* he loved and gave me a copy which I still possess.) Another good translation was brought out by John Jackson in 1906, which reads smoothly enough – apart from its rather self-consciously 'literary language' – but to my mind is disfigured by the very unsympathetic view taken of Marcus himself in the introductory essay by C. Bigg. The closely accurate version by C. R. Haines (1915) in the Loeb series, though probably indispensable to students who want an exact rendering of the Greek, hardly lends itself to being read for pleasure.[1]

Excellent in their different ways, these translations have held the field against a number of lesser rivals for a long time. But it is nearly half-a-century now since the last of them made its appearance, and to younger eyes they have undeniably come to look a little stiff-jointed. It would be a great pity if this were to keep a new generation from discovering for itself the humane wisdom and gentle charm of Marcus Aurelius; and it is therefore in the modest hope of doing something to avert such a misfortune that this present version has been made.

It should be added that there is no attempt here to reproduce the curious prose style of the original. I have an idea that

1. As a fine example of more recent scholarship, nothing is more admirable than the two comprehensive volumes of A. S. L. Farquharson's critical edition of the *Meditations*, published in 1944 and including a translation. A work of this size, scope and cost, however, is meant for a different class of readers.

writing in Greek did not come very easily to Marcus the Roman; his expressions are often obscure, and he uses awkward and unusual constructions. At the same time his language has dignity, and his vocabulary is that of an educated man. Something like the limpid and beautiful English of John Henry Newman (between whom and Marcus there are manifest affinities) is needed to do justice to the spiritual qualities of the *Meditations*. I could not hope to achieve this, so I have aimed at nothing more than a plain and honest version for the Greekless reader.

My best thanks are due to my friend Henry Neill for his kindness in reading the manuscript and making many valuable suggestions for its improvement. I am also most grateful for Dr E. V. Rieu's generous encouragement and advice and the measure of my debt to his assistant on the editorial staff, Mrs Betty Radice, for her help and counsel in preparing the book for press can only be gauged by those who have had the benefit of her sympathetic interest and acute scholarship.

MAXWELL STANIFORTH

Sixpenny Hundley, 1962

BOOK ONE

1. Courtesy and serenity of temper I first learnt to know from my grandfather Verus.

2. Manliness without ostentation I learnt from what I have heard and remember of my father.

3. My mother set me an example of piety and generosity, avoidance of all uncharitableness – not in actions only, but in thought as well – and a simplicity of life quite unlike the usual habits of the rich.

4. To my great-grandfather I owed the advice to dispense with the education of the schools and have good masters at home instead – and to realize that no expense should be grudged for this purpose.

5. It was my tutor who dissuaded me from patronizing Green or Blue [1] at the races, or Light or Heavy [2] in the ring; and encouraged me not to be afraid of work, to be sparing in my wants, attend to my own needs, mind my own business, and never listen to gossip.

6. Thanks to Diognetus [3] I learnt not to be absorbed in trivial pursuits; to be sceptical of wizards and wonder-workers with

1. The colours of the rival charioteers in the Circus. Roman enthusiasm for these races was unbounded; successful drivers earned large fortunes and became popular idols.

2. In one form of gladiatorial combat (the 'Thracian') the opponents were armed with light round bucklers; in another (the 'Samnite') they carried heavy oblong shields.

3. The painter and philosopher to whom Marcus, as a boy of eleven, owed his first acquaintance with Stoicism. Nothing is known of Bacchius, Tandasis, or Marcian.

their tales of spells, exorcisms, and the like; to eschew cock-fighting and other such distractions; not to resent outspokenness; to familiarize myself with philosophy, beginning with Bacchius and going on to Tandasis and Marcian; to write compositions in my early years; and to be ardent for the plank-and-skin pallet and other rigours of the Greek discipline.

7. From Rusticus [1] I derived the notion that my character needed training and care, and that I must not allow myself to be led astray into a sophist's enthusiasm for concocting speculative treatises, edifying homilies, or imaginary sketches of The Ascetic or The Altruist. He also taught me to avoid rhetoric, poetry, and verbal conceits, affectations of dress at home, and other such lapses of taste, and to imitate the easy epistolary style of his own letter written at Sinuessa to my mother. If anyone, after falling out with me in a moment of temper, showed signs of wanting to make peace again, I was to be ready at once to meet them half-way. Also I was to be accurate in my reading, and not content with a mere general idea of the meaning; and not to let myself be too quickly convinced by a glib tongue. Through him, too, I came to know Epictetus's *Dissertations*, of which he gave me a copy from his library.

8. Apollonius [2] impressed on me the need to make decisions for myself instead of depending on the hazards of chance, and never for a moment to leave reason out of sight. He also schooled me to meet spasms of acute pain, the loss of my son, and the tedium of a chronic ailment with the same unaltered

1. Q. Junius Rusticus, a Stoic professor who was the law-tutor and friend of Marcus.

2. A teacher of philosophy who came to Rome from Chalcedon. When first summoned by Marcus to the palace, he is said to have replied, 'The master ought not to come to the pupil, but the pupil to the master.'

composure. He himself was a living proof that
energy is not incompatible with the ability to relax
sitions were always a model of clarity; yet he was evidently
one who rated practical experience and an aptitude for teaching philosophy as the least of his accomplishments. It was he,
moreover, who taught me how to accept the pretended favours
of friends without either lowering my own self-respect or
giving the impression of an unfeeling indifference.

9. My debts to Sextus [1] include kindliness, how to rule a
household with paternal authority, the real meaning of the
Natural Life, an unselfconscious dignity, an intuitive concern
for the interests of one's friends, and a good-natured patience
with amateurs and visionaries. The aptness of his courtesy to
each individual lent a charm to his society more potent than
any flattery, yet at the same time it exacted the complete respect of all present. His manner, too, of determining and
systematizing the essential rules of life was as comprehensive
as it was methodical. Never displaying a sign of anger nor
any kind of emotion, he was at once entirely imperturbable
and yet full of kindly affection. His approval was always
quietly and undemonstratively expressed, and he never
paraded his encyclopaedic learning.

10. It was the critic Alexander [2] who put me on my guard
against unnecessary fault-finding. People should not be
sharply corrected for bad grammar, provincialisms, or mis-
pronunciation; it is better to suggest the proper expression by
tactfully introducing it oneself in, say, one's reply to a question or one's acquiescence in their sentiments, or into a
friendly discussion of the topic itself (not of the diction), or
by some other suitable form of reminder.

1. A native of Chaeronea in Boeotia and the grandson of Plutarch.
One of Marcus's earliest instructors in philosophy.

2. A Greek and a scholar of repute, known as 'the Grammarian'.

11. To my mentor Fronto [1] I owe the realization that malice, craftiness, and duplicity are the concomitants of absolute power; and that our patrician families tend for the most part to be lacking in the feelings of ordinary humanity.

12. Alexander the Platonist [2] cautioned me against frequent use of the words 'I am too busy' in speech or correspondence, except in cases of real necessity; saying that no one ought to shirk the obligations due to society on the excuse of urgent affairs.

13. Catulus the Stoic [3] counselled me never to make light of a friend's rebuke, even when unreasonable, but to do my best to restore myself to his good graces; to speak up readily in commendation of my instructors, as we read in the memoirs of Domitius and Athenodotus; and to cultivate a genuine affection for my children.

14. From my brother Severus [4] I learnt to love my relations, to

1. M. Cornelius Fronto, a celebrated pleader and teacher of rhetoric and reckoned inferior only to Cicero as an orator. He was entrusted with the education of the future co-emperors Marcus Aurelius and Lucius Verus. The published edition of Fronto's correspondence, containing many of his letters to them and their replies, throws much incidental light on the character and habits of Marcus, and also reveals the affection in which both his royal pupils held their tutor.

2. The emperor's secretary.

3. Cinna Catulus was another of the professors who gave lectures in philosophy.

4. Marcus had no brother. The word may be a playful allusion to Claudius Severus (whose son married one of Marcus's daughters), since Marcus also had originally been called Severus, though he later discarded the name. More probably the text is corrupt. Many editors prefer to read Verus, that is the Lucius Verus who, like Marcus himself, had been adopted by the emperor Antoninus Pius as his son; but the flattering picture drawn here by no means corresponds with what is known of the character of Verus (see note 1 on p. 42).

love the truth, and to love justice. Through him I came to know of Thrasea, Cato, Helvidius, Dion, and Brutus, and became acquainted with the conception of a community based on equality and freedom of speech for all, and a monarchy concerned primarily to uphold the liberty of the subject. He showed me the need for a fair and dispassionate appreciation of philosophy, an addiction to good works, open-handedness, a sanguine temper, and confidence in the affection of my friends. I remember, too, his forthrightness with those who came under his censure, and his way of leaving his friends in no doubt of his likes and dislikes, but of telling them plainly.

15. Maximus [1] was my model for self-control, fixity of purpose, and cheerfulness under ill-health or other misfortunes. His character was an admirable combination of dignity and charm, and all the duties of his station were performed quietly and without fuss. He gave everyone the conviction that he spoke as he believed, and acted as he judged right. Bewilderment or timidity were unknown to him; he was never hasty, never dilatory; nothing found him at a loss. He indulged neither in despondency nor forced gaiety, nor had anger or jealousy any power over him. Kindliness, sympathy, and sincerity all contributed to give the impression of a rectitude that was innate rather than inculcated. Nobody was ever made by him to feel inferior, yet none could have presumed to challenge his pre-eminence. He was also the possessor of an agreeable sense of humour.

16. The qualities I admired in my father [2] were his lenience,

1. Claudius Maximus, a Stoic philosopher especially admired by Marcus. His courage in sickness is appreciatively recalled (1, 16) and his death and that of his wife Secunda remembered with regret (VIII, 25).
2. Not his natural father Annius Verus, but the emperor Antoninus Pius, his adoptive father.

his firm refusal to be diverted from any decision he had deliberately reached, his complete indifference to meretricious
honours; his industry, perseverance, and willingness to listen
to any project for the common good; the unvarying insistence
that rewards must depend on merit; the expert's sense of
when to tighten the reins and when to relax them; and the
efforts he made to suppress pederasty.

He was aware that social life must have its claims: his
friends were under no obligation to join him at his table or
attend his progresses, and when they were detained by other
engagements it made no difference to him. Every question
that came before him in council was painstakingly and
patiently examined; he was never content to dismiss it on a
cursory first impression. His friendships were enduring; they
were not capricious, and they were not extravagant. He was
always equal to an occasion; cheerful, yet long-sighted enough
to have all his dispositions unobtrusively perfected down to
the last detail. He had an ever-watchful eye to the needs of
the Empire, prudently conserving its resources and putting up
with the criticisms that resulted. Before his gods he was not
superstitious; before his fellow-men he never stooped to bid
for popularity or woo the masses, but pursued his own calm
and steady way, disdaining anything that savoured of the
flashy or new-fangled. He accepted without either complacency or compunction such material comforts as fortune had
put at his disposal; when they were to hand he would avail
himself of them frankly, but when they were not he had no
regrets.

Not a vestige of the casuist's quibbling, the lackey's pert-
ness, the pedant's over-scrupulosity could be charged against
him; all men recognized in him a mature and finished per-
sonality, that was impervious to flattery and entirely capable
of ruling both himself and others. Moreover, he had a high

respect for all genuine philosophers; and though refraining from criticism of the rest, he preferred to dispense with their guidance. In society he was affable and gracious without being fulsome. The care he took of his body was reasonable; there was no solicitous anxiety to prolong its existence, or to embellish its appearance, yet he was far from unmindful of it, and indeed looked after himself so successfully that he was seldom in need of medical attention or physic or liniments. No hint of jealousy showed in his prompt recognition of outstanding abilities, whether in public speaking, law, ethics, or any other department, and he took pains to give each man the chance of earning a reputation in his own field. Though all his actions were guided by a respect for constitutional precedent, he would never go out of his way to court public recognition of this. Again, he disliked restlessness and change, and had a rooted preference for the same places and the same pursuits. After one of his acute spasms of migraine he would lose no time in taking up his normal duties again, with new vigour and complete command of his powers. His secret and confidential files were not numerous, and the few infrequent items in them referred exclusively to matters of state. He showed good sense and restraint over the exhibition of spectacles, construction of public buildings, distribution of subsidies, and so forth, having always more in view the necessity for the measures themselves than the plaudits they evoked. His baths were not taken at inconvenient hours; he had no mania for building; he was quite uncritical of the food he ate, of the cut and colour of the garments he wore, or of the personableness of those around him. His clothes were sent up from his country seat at Lorium, and most of his things came from Lanuvium. His well-known treatment of the apologetic overseer at Tusculum was typical of his whole behaviour, for discourtesy was as foreign to his nature as harshness or bluster; he never grew heated, as the saying is, to sweating-point; it was his habit to analyse and weigh every incident, taking his time about it, calmly, methodically, decisively, and consistently. What is recorded of Socrates was no less applicable to him, that he had the ability to allow or deny himself indulgences which most people are as much incapacitated by their weakness from refusing as by their excesses from appreciating. To be thus strong enough to refrain or consent at will argues a consummate and indomitable soul – as Maximus also demonstrated on his sick-bed.

17. To the gods I owe good grandparents, good parents, a good sister, and teachers, comrades, kinsmen, and friends good almost without exception; and that I never fell out with any of them, in spite of a temperament that could very well have precipitated something of the sort, had not circumstances providentially never combined to put me to the proof. To them, too, I owe it that the responsibility of my grandfather's mistress for my upbringing was brought to an early end, and my innocence preserved; and that I was not impatient to reach manhood, but contented myself with an unhurried development. I thank heaven also that under my father the Emperor I was cured of all pomposity, and made to realize that life at court can be lived without royal escorts, robes of state, illuminations, statues, and outward splendour of that kind, but that one's manner of life can be reduced almost to the level of a private gentleman's without losing the prestige and authority needful when affairs of state require leadership. The gods, too, gave me a brother [1] whose natural

1. This was Lucius Ceionius Commodus, afterwards known as Lucius Verus. He was adopted by Antoninus Pius along with Marcus, with whom he was associated as co-emperor and whose daughter Lucilla he married. Originally a man of courage and ability, Verus degenerated into weakness and self-indulgence. As commander of the Roman

qualities were a standing challenge to my own self-discipline at the same time as his deferential affection warmed my heart; and children who were neither intellectually stunted nor physically misshapen. It was the gods who set a limit to my proficiency in rhetoric, poetry, and other studies that might well have absorbed my time, had I found it less difficult to make progress. They saw to it that at the first opportunity I raised my tutors to such rank and station as I thought they had at heart, instead of putting them off with prospects of later advancement on the plea of their youth. To the gods I owe my acquaintance with Apollonius, Rusticus, and Maximus. To them, too, my vivid and recurrent visions of the true inwardness of the Natural Life; indeed, for their part, the favours, helps, and inspirations I have received leave my failure to attain this Natural Life without excuse; and if I am still far from the goal, the fault is my own for not paying heed to the reminders – nay, the virtual directions – which I have had from above.

To the gods it must be ascribed that my constitution has survived this manner of life so long; that I never got entangled with a Benedicta nor a Theodotus, and also emerged from other subsequent affairs unscathed; that although Rusticus and I frequently had our differences, I never pushed things to a point I might have regretted; and that the last years of my mother's life, before her early death, were spent with me. Futhermore, that on occasions when I thought of relieving somebody in poverty or distress, I was never told that I had not the necessary means; as also that I myself never had

armies in the Parthian war he proved indolent and incapable, and was only saved from disgrace by the skill of his generals. When he returned with his legions from the East, they carried back the seeds of a pestilence which spread with terrible effect throughout the Empire. Verus died in 169 – as some said, by the hand of a poisoner.

occasion to require similar help from another. And I must thank heaven for such a wife as mine, so submissive, so loving, and so artless; for an unfailing supply of competent tutors for my children; and for remedies prescribed for me in dreams – especially in cases of blood-spitting and vertigo, as happened at Caieta and Chrysa. Finally, that with all my addiction to philosophy I was yet preserved from either falling a prey to some sophist or spending all my time at a desk poring over textbooks and rules of logic or grinding at natural science.

For all these good things 'man needs the help of Heaven and Destiny'.*

Among the Quadi, on the River Gran.

---

* Apparently a quotation, the source of which has not been traced.

BOOK TWO

1. Begin each day by telling yourself: Today I shall be meeting with interference, ingratitude, insolence, disloyalty, ill-will, and selfishness – all of them due to the offenders' ignorance of what is good or evil. But for my part I have long perceived the nature of good and its nobility, the nature of evil and its meanness, and also the nature of the culprit himself, who is my brother (not in the physical sense, but as a fellow-creature similarly endowed with reason and a share of the divine); therefore none of those things can injure me, for nobody can implicate me in what is degrading. Neither can I be angry with my brother or fall foul of him; for he and I were born to work together, like a man's two hands, feet, or eyelids, or like the upper and lower rows of his teeth. To obstruct each other is against Nature's law – and what is irritation or aversion but a form of obstruction?

2. A little flesh, a little breath, and a Reason to rule all – that is myself. (Forget your books; no more hankering for them; they were no part of your equipment.) As one already on the threshold of death, think nothing of the first – of its viscid blood, its bones, its web of nerves and veins and arteries. The breath, too; what is that? A whiff of wind; and not even the same wind, but every moment puffed out and drawn in anew. But the third, the Reason, the master – on this you must concentrate. Now that your hairs are grey, let it play the part of a slave no more, twitching puppetwise at every pull of self-interest; and cease to fume at destiny by ever grumbling at today or lamenting over tomorrow.

3. The whole divine economy is pervaded by Providence.

...e vagaries of chance have their place in Nature's
...; that is, in the intricate tapestry of the ordinances of
Providence. Providence is the source from which all things
flow; and allied with it is Necessity, and the welfare of the
universe. You yourself are a part of that universe; and for
any one of nature's parts, that which is assigned to it by the
World-Nature or helps to keep it in being is good. Moreover,
what keeps the whole world in being is Change: not merely
change of the basic elements, but also change of the larger
formations they compose. On these thoughts rest content, and
ever hold them as principles. Forget your thirst for books; so
that when your end comes you may not murmur, but meet it
with a good grace and with unfeigned gratitude in your heart
to the gods.

4. Think of your many years of procrastination; how the
gods have repeatedly granted you further periods of grace, of
which you have taken no advantage. It is time now to realize
the nature of the universe to which you belong, and of that
controlling Power whose offspring you are; and to understand that your time has a limit set to it. Use it, then, to
advance your enlightenment; or it will be gone, and never
in your power again.

5. Hour by hour resolve firmly, like a Roman and a man, to
do what comes to hand with correct and natural dignity, and
with humanity, independence, and justice. Allow your mind
freedom from all other considerations. This you can do, if
you will approach each action as though it were your last,
dismissing the wayward thought, the emotional recoil from
the commands of reason, the desire to create an impression,
the admiration of self, the discontent with your lot. See how
little a man needs to master, for his days to flow on in quiet-

ness and piety : he has but to observe these few counsels, and the gods will ask nothing more.

6. Wrong, wrong thou art doing to thyself, O my soul; and all too soon thou shalt have no more time to do thyself right. Man has but one life; already thine is nearing its close, yet still hast thou no eye to thine own honour, but art staking thy happiness on the souls of other men.[1]

7. Are you distracted by outward cares? Then allow yourself a space of quiet, wherein you can add to your knowledge of the Good and learn to curb your restlessness. Guard also against another kind of error : the folly of those who weary their days in much business, but lack any aim on which their whole effort, nay, their whole thought, is focussed.

8. You will not easily find a man coming to grief through indifference to the workings of another's soul; but for those who pay no heed to the motions of their own, unhappiness is their sure reward.

9. Remembering always what the World-Nature is, and what my own nature is, and how the one stands in respect to the other – so small a fraction of so vast a Whole – bear in mind that no man can hinder you from conforming each word and deed to that Nature of which you are a part.

10. When Theophrastus is comparing sins – so far as they are commonly acknowledged to be comparable – he affirms the philosophic truth that sins of desire are more culpable than sins of passion. For passion's revulsion from reason at least seems to bring with it a certain discomfort, and a half-felt sense of constraint; whereas sins of desire, in which pleasure predominates, indicate a more self-indulgent and

1. That is, on whether others decide to approve or censure your actions.

disposition. Both experience and philosophy, then,
e contention that a sin which is pleasurable deserves
graver censure than one which is painful. In the one case the
offender is like a man stung into an involuntary loss of control by some injustice; in the other, eagerness to gratify his
desire moves him to do wrong of his own volition.

11. In all you do or say or think, recollect that at any time
the power of withdrawal from life is in your own hands. If
gods exist, you have nothing to fear in taking leave of mankind, for they will not let you come to harm. But if there
are no gods, or if they have no concern with mortal affairs,
what is life to me, in a world devoid of gods or devoid of
Providence? Gods, however, do exist, and do concern themselves with the world of men. They have given us full power
not to fall into any of the absolute evils; and if there were
real evil in life's other experiences, they would have provided
for that too, so that avoidance of it could lie within every
man's ability. But when a thing does not worsen the man
himself, how can it worsen the life he lives? The World-
Nature cannot have been so ignorant as to overlook a hazard
of this kind, nor, if aware of it, have been unable to devise
a safeguard or a remedy. Neither want of power nor want of
skill could have led Nature into the error of allowing good
and evil to be visited indiscriminately on the virtuous and the
sinful alike. Yet living and dying, honour and dishonour,
pain and pleasure, riches and poverty, and so forth are equally
the lot of good men and bad. Things like these neither ele-
vate nor degrade; and therefore they are no more good than
they are evil.

12. Our mental powers should enable us to perceive the
swiftness with which all things vanish away: their bodies
in the world of space, and their remembrance in the world

of time. We should also observe the nature of all objects of sense – particularly such as allure us with pleasure, or affright us with pain, or are clamorously urged upon us by the voice of self-conceit – the cheapness and contemptibility of them, how sordid they are, and how quickly fading and dead. We should discern the true worth of those whose word and opinion confer reputations. We should apprehend, too, the nature of death; and that if only it be steadily contemplated, and the fancies we associate with it be mentally dissected, it will soon come to be thought of as no more than a process of nature (and only children are scared by a natural process) – or rather, something more than a mere process, a positive contribution to nature's well-being. Also we can learn how man has contact with God, and with which part of himself this is maintained, and how that part fares after its removal hence.

13. Nothing is more melancholy than to compass the whole creation, 'probing into the deeps of earth', as the poet says, and peering curiously into the secrets of others' souls, without once understanding that to hold fast to the divine spirit within, and serve it loyally, is all that is needful. Such service involves keeping it pure from passion, and from aimlessness, and from discontent with the works of gods or men; for the former of these works deserve our reverence, for their excellence; the latter our goodwill, for fraternity's sake, and at times perhaps our pity too, because of men's ignorance of good and evil – an infirmity as crippling as the inability to distinguish black from white.

14. Were you to live three thousand years, or even thirty thousand, remember that the sole life which a man can lose is that which he is living at the moment; and furthermore, that he can have no other life except the one he loses. This

means that the longest life and the shortest amount to the same thing. For the passing minute is every man's equal possession, but what has once gone by is not ours. Our loss, therefore, is limited to that one fleeting instant, since no one can lose what is already past, nor yet what is still to come – for how can he be deprived of what he does not possess? So two things should be borne in mind. First, that all the cycles of creation since the beginning of time exhibit the same recurring pattern, so that it can make no difference whether you watch the identical spectacle for a hundred years, or for two hundred, or for ever. Secondly, that when the longest- and the shortest-lived of us come to die, their loss is precisely equal. For the sole thing of which any man can be deprived is the present; since this is all he owns, and nobody can lose what is not his.

15. There are obvious objections to the Cynic Monimus's statement that 'things are determined by the view taken of them'; but the value of his aphorism is equally obvious, if we admit the substance of it so far as it contains a truth.

16. For a human soul, the greatest of self-inflicted wrongs is to make itself (so far as it is able to do so) a kind of tumour or abscess on the universe; for to quarrel with circumstances is always a rebellion against Nature – and Nature includes the nature of each individual part. Another wrong, again, is to reject a fellow-creature or oppose him with malicious intent, as men do when they are angry. A third, to surrender to pleasure or pain. A fourth, to dissemble and show insincerity or falsity in word or deed. A fifth, for the soul to direct its acts and endeavours to no particular object, and waste its energies purposelessly and without due thought; for even the least of our activities ought to have some end in view – and for

creatures with reason, that end is conformity with the reason and law of the primordial City and Commonwealth.

17. <u>In the life of a man, his time is but a moment</u>, his being an incessant flux, his senses a dim rushlight, his body a prey of worms, his soul an unquiet eddy, his fortune dark, and his fame doubtful. In short, all that is of the body is as coursing waters, all that is of the soul as dreams and vapours; life a warfare, a brief sojourning in an alien land; and after repute, oblivion. Where, then, can man find the power to guide and guard his steps? In one thing and one alone: Philosophy. To be a philosopher is to keep unsullied and unscathed the divine spirit within him, so that it may transcend all pleasure and all pain, take nothing in hand without purpose and nothing falsely or with dissimulation, depend not on another's actions or inactions, accept each and every dispensation as coming from the same Source as itself – and last and chief, wait with a good grace for death, as no more than a simple dissolving of the elements whereof each living thing is composed. If those elements themselves take no harm from their ceaseless forming and re-forming, why look with mistrust upon the change and dissolution of the whole? It is but Nature's way; and in the ways of Nature there is no evil to be found.

BOOK THREE

1. The daily wearing away of life, with its ever-shrinking remainder, is not the only thing we have to consider. For even if a man's years be prolonged, we must still take into account that it is doubtful whether his mind will continue to retain its capacity for the understanding of business, or for the contemplative effort needed to apprehend things divine and human. The onset of senility may involve no loss of respiratory or alimentary powers, or of sensations, impulses and so forth; nevertheless, the ability to make full use of his faculties, to assess correctly the demands of duty, to coordinate all the diverse problems that arise, to judge if the time has come to end his days on earth, or to make any other of the decisions that require the exercise of a practised intellect, is already on the wane. We must press on, then, in haste; not simply because every hour brings us nearer to death, but because even before then our powers of perception and comprehension begin to deteriorate.

Another thing we should remark is the grace and fascination that there is even in the incidentals of Nature's processes. When a loaf of bread, for instance, is in the oven, cracks appear in it here and there; and these flaws, though not intended in the baking, have a rightness of their own, and sharpen the appetite. Figs, again, at their ripest will also crack open. When olives are on the verge of falling, the very imminence of decay adds its peculiar beauty to the fruit. So, too, the drooping head of a cornstalk, the wrinkling skin when a lion scowls, the drip of foam from a wild boar's jaws, and many more such sights, are far from beautiful if looked at by themselves; yet as the consequences of some other process of Nature, they make their own contribution to its charm and attractiveness.

2. Thus to a man of sensitiveness and sufficiently deep insight into the workings of the universe, almost everything, even if it be no more than a by-product of something else, seems to add its meed of extra pleasure. Such a man will view the grinning jaws of real lions and tigers as admiringly as he would an artist's or sculptor's imitation of them; and the eye of discretion will enable him to see the mature charm that belongs to men and women in old age, as well as the seductive bloom that is youth's. Things of this sort will not appeal to everyone; he alone who has cultivated a real intimacy with Nature and her works will be struck by them.

3. Hippocrates [1] cured the ills of many, but himself took ill and died. The Chaldeans foretold the deaths of many, but fate caught up with them also. Alexander, Pompey, and Julius Caesar laid waste whole cities time and again, and cut down many thousands of horse and foot in battle, but the hour came when they too passed away. Heraclitus [2] speculated

1. Hippocrates (c. 460–355 B.C.) was a native of the island of Cos and the most celebrated physician of antiquity. His numerous treatises formed the subsequent groundwork of all medical science in the classical world. There seems little reason to doubt the ascription to him of the 'Hippocratic oath'; and he is also credited with the authorship of the saying, 'Life is short, art is long.'

2. Heraclitus (c. 540–475 B.C.), an Ionian philosopher, taught that the essence of Being is Becoming: i.e. an incessant movement of change, by which one aspect of a thing is always leading on to another. The type of this perpetual movement, and the primordial form of all matter, is fire; and the elemental process of the universe is a passage from fire through water and earth back to fire again. 'All things are in flux' and 'You cannot step into the same river twice' were two of the well-known sayings in which he expressed his doctrine; and some others are recalled by Marcus in IV, 46. Much of the later Stoic system of physics was based on the theories of Heraclitus.

endlessly on the consumption of the universe by fire, but in the end it was water that saturated his body, and he died in a dung-plaster. Democritus [1] was destroyed by vermin; Socrates by vermin of another kind. [2] And the moral of it all? This. You embark; you make the voyage; you reach port: step ashore, then. Into another life? There are gods everywhere, even yonder. Into final insensibility? Then you will be out of the grip of pains and pleasures, and thrall no longer to this earthen vessel, so immeasurably meaner than its attendant minister. For the one is a mind and a divinity; the other but clay and corruption.

4. Do not waste what remains of your life in speculating about your neighbours, unless with a view to some mutual benefit. To wonder what so-and-so is doing and why, or what he is saying, or thinking, or scheming – in a word, anything that distracts you from fidelity to the Ruler within you – means a loss of opportunity for some other task. See then that the flow of your thoughts is kept free from idle or random fancies, particularly those of an inquisitive or uncharitable nature. A man should habituate himself to such a way of thinking that if suddenly asked, 'What is in your mind at this minute?' he could respond frankly and without

1. Democritus, a contemporary of Hippocrates, maintained that the universe was formed by the infinitely various combinations of infinite numbers of atoms; a belief in which he was afterwards followed by Epicurus and his school. In contrast to the gloomy Heraclitus, the 'weeping philosopher', his cheerful disposition earned him the nickname of the 'laughing philosopher'. Marcus is our only authority for this version of his death.

2. The allusion is to Melitus the poet, Anytus the tanner, and Lycon the orator. They brought the charge against Socrates for which he was condemned to death. Soon after his execution the Athenians repented of their injustice, stoned Melitus to death, and banished Anytus and Lycon.

hesitation; thus proving that all his thoughts were simple and kindly, as becomes a social being with no taste for the pleasures of sensual imaginings, jealousies, envies, suspicions, or any other sentiments that he would blush to acknowledge in himself. Such a man, determined here and now to aspire to the heights, is indeed a priest and minister of the gods; for he is making full use of that indwelling power which can keep a man unsullied by pleasures, proof against pain, untouched by insult, and impervious to evil. He is a competitor in the greatest of all contests, the struggle against passion's mastery; he is imbued through and through with uprightness, welcoming whole-heartedly whatever falls to his lot and rarely asking himself what others may be saying or doing or thinking except when the public interest requires it. He confines his operations to his own concerns, having his attention fixed on his own particular thread of the universal web; seeing to it that his actions are honourable, and convinced that what befalls him must be for the best – for his own directing fate is itself under a higher direction. He does not forget the brotherhood of all rational beings, nor that a concern for every man is proper to humanity; and he knows that it is not the world's opinions he should follow, but only those of men whose lives confessedly accord with Nature. As for others whose lives are not so ordered, he reminds himself constantly of the characters they exhibit daily and nightly at home and abroad, and of the sort of society they frequent; and the approval of such men, who do not even stand well in their own eyes, has no value for him.

5. In your actions let there be a willing promptitude, yet a regard for the common interest; due deliberation, yet no irresolution; and in your sentiments no pretentious over-refinement. Avoid talkativeness, avoid officiousness. The god

within you should preside over a being who is virile
mature, a statesman, a Roman, and a ruler; one who has held
his ground, like a soldier waiting for the signal to retire from
life's battlefield and ready to welcome his relief; a man whose
credit need neither be sworn to by himself nor avouched by
others. Therein is the secret of cheerfulness, of depending on
no help from without and needing to crave from no man the
boon of tranquillity. We have to stand upright ourselves, not
be set up.

6. If mortal life can offer you anything better than justice and
truth, self-control and courage – that is, peace of mind in the
evident conformity of your actions to the laws of reason, and
peace of mind under the visitations of a destiny you cannot
control – if, I say, you can discern any higher ideal, why, turn
to it with your whole soul, and rejoice in the prize you have
found. But if nothing seems to you better than the deity
which dwells within you, directing each impulse, weighing
each impression, abjuring (in the Socratic phrase) the tempta-
tions of the flesh, and avowing allegiance to the gods and
compassion for mankind; if you find all else to be mean and
worthless in comparison, then leave yourself no room for
any rival pursuits. For if you once falter and turn aside, you
will no longer be able to give unswerving loyalty to this ideal
you have chosen for your own. No ambitions of a different
nature can contest the title to goodness which belongs to
reason and civic duty; not the world's applause, nor power,
nor wealth, nor the enjoyment of pleasure. For a while there
may seem to be no incongruity in these things, but very
quickly they get the upper hand and sweep a man off his
balance. Do you then, I would say, simply and spontaneously
make your choice of the highest, and cleave to that. 'But
what is best for myself is the highest,' you say? If it is best

for you as a reasonable being, hold fast to it; but if as an animal merely, then say so outright, and maintain your view with becoming humility – only be very sure that you have probed the matter aright.

7. Never value the advantages derived from anything involving breach of faith, loss of self-respect, hatred, suspicion, or execration of others, insincerity, or the desire for something which has to be veiled and curtained. One whose chief regard is for his own mind, and for the divinity within him and the service of its goodness, will strike no poses, utter no complaints, and crave neither for solitude nor yet for a crowd. Best of all, his life will be free from continual pursuings and avoidings. He does not care whether his soul in its mortal frame shall be his to possess for a longer or a shorter term of years; this very moment, if it be the hour for his departure, he will step forth as readily as he performs any other act that can be done in self-respecting and orderly fashion. No other care has he in life but to keep his mind from straying into paths incompatible with those of an intelligent and social being.

8. In a mind that is disciplined and purified there is no taint of corruption, no unclean spot nor festering sore. Such a man's life fate can never snatch away unfulfilled, as it were an actor walking off in mid-performance before the play is finished. There is nothing of the lackey in him, yet nothing of the coxcomb; he neither leans on others nor holds aloof from them; and he remains answerable to no man, yet guiltless of all evasion.

9. Treat with respect the power you have to form an opinion. By it alone can the helmsman within you avoid forming opinions that are at variance with nature and with the constitution of a reasonable being. From it you may look to attain

circumspection, good relations with your fellow-men, and conformity with the will of heaven.

10. Letting go all else, cling to the following few truths. Remember that man lives only in the present, in this fleeting instant: all the rest of his life is either past and gone, or not yet revealed. This mortal life is a little thing, lived in a little corner of the earth; and little, too, is the longest fame to come – dependent as it is on a succession of fast-perishing little men who have no knowledge even of their own selves, much less of one long dead and gone.

11. To these maxims add yet another. When an object presents itself to your perception, make a mental definition or at least an outline of it, so as to discern its essential character, to pierce beyond its separate attributes to a distinct view of the naked whole, and to identify for yourself both the object itself and the elements of which it is composed, and into which it will again be resolved. Nothing so enlarges the mind as this ability to examine methodically and accurately every one of life's experiences, with an eye to determining its classification, the ends it serves, its worth to the universe, and its worth to men as the members of that supreme City in which all other cities are as households. Take, for example, the thing which is producing its impression upon me at this moment. What is it? Whereof is it composed? How long is it designed to last? What moral response does it ask of me; gentleness, fortitude, candour, good faith, sincerity, self-reliance, or some other quality? In every instance learn to say, This comes from God; or, This is one of Fate's dispensations, a strand in the complex web, a conjunction of fortuities; or again, This is the work of a man who is of the same stock and breed and brotherhood as I am, but is ignorant of what Nature requires of him. I myself, however, can plead no such ignorance,

and therefore in accordance with Nature's law of brotherhood I am to deal amiably and fairly with him – though
at the same time, if there be no question of good or evil
involved, I must aim my shafts at the proper merits of the
case.

12. If you do the task before you always adhering to strict
reason with zeal and energy and yet with humanity, disregarding all lesser ends and keeping the divinity within you
pure and upright, as though you were even now faced with
its recall – if you hold steadily to this, staying for nothing
and shrinking from nothing, only seeking in each passing
action a conformity with nature and in each word and utterance a fearless truthfulness, then shall the good life be yours.
And from this course no man has the power to hold you back.

13. As surgeons keep their lancets and scalpels always at
hand for the sudden demands of their craft, so keep your
principles constantly in readiness for the understanding of
things both human and divine; never in the most trivial
action forgetting how intimately the two are related. For
nothing human can be done aright without reference to the
divine, and conversely.

14. Mislead yourself no longer; you will never read these
notebooks again now, nor the annals of bygone Romans and
Greeks, nor that choice selection of writings you have put
by for your old age. Press on, then, to the finish; cast away
vain hopes; and if you have any regard at all for self, see to
your own security while still you may.

15. They do not know all that is signified by such words as
'stealing', 'sowing', 'purchasing', 'being at peace', 'seeing
one's duty' : this needs a different vision from the eye's.

16. Body, soul, and mind: the body for sensation, the soul for the springs of action, the mind for principles. Yet the capacity for sensation belongs also to the stalled ox; there is no wild beast, homosexual, Nero, or Phalaris [1] but obeys the twitchings of impulse; and even men who deny the gods, or betray their country, or perpetrate all manner of villainy behind locked doors, have minds to guide them to the clear path of duty. Seeing, then, that all else is the common heritage of such types, the good man's only singularity lies in his approving welcome to every experience the looms of fate may weave for him, his refusal to soil the divinity seated in his breast or perturb it with disorderly impressions, and his resolve to keep it in serenity and decorous obedience to God, admitting no disloyalty to truth in his speech or to justice in his actions. Though all the world mistrust him because he lives in simple, self-respecting happiness, he takes offence at none, but unswervingly treads the road onward to life's close, where duty bids him arrive in purity and peace, unreluctant to depart, in perfect and unforced unison with fate's apportionment.

1. Phalaris, ruler of Agrigentum in Sicily in the sixth century B.C., earned a proverbial reputation by his inhuman cruelty. He is said to have burnt his captives alive in a brazen bull, the first victim being its inventor Perillus. The spurious 'Epistles of Phalaris' are now remembered chiefly in connexion with the English scholar Richard Bentley, who proved them to be forgeries in the 'immortal Dissertation' (Porson) which established his reputation.

BOOK FOUR

1. If the inward power that rules us be true to Nature, it will always adjust itself readily to the possibilities and opportunities offered by circumstance. It asks for no predeterminate material; in the pursuance of its aims it is willing to compromise; hindrances to its progress are merely converted into matter for its own use. It is like a bonfire mastering a heap of rubbish, which would have quenched a feeble glow; but its fiery blaze quickly assimilates the load, consumes it, and flames the higher for it.

2. Take no enterprise in hand at haphazard, or without regard to the principles governing its proper execution.

3. Men seek for seclusion in the wilderness, by the seashore, or in the mountains – a dream you have cherished only too fondly yourself. But such fancies are wholly unworthy of a philosopher, since at any moment you choose you can retire within yourself. Nowhere can man find a quieter or more untroubled retreat than in his own soul; above all, he who possesses resources in himself, which he need only contemplate to secure immediate ease of mind – the ease that is but another word for a well-ordered spirit. Avail yourself often, then, of this retirement, and so continually renew yourself. Make your rules of life brief, yet so as to embrace the fundamentals; recurrence to them will then suffice to remove all vexation, and send you back without fretting to the duties to which you must return.

After all, what is it that frets you? The vices of humanity? Remember the doctrine that all rational beings are created for one another; that toleration is a part of justice; and that men are not intentional evildoers. Think of the myriad

63

picions, animosities, and conflicts that are now
the dust and ashes of the men who knew them;
ore.

Or is it your allotted portion in the universe that chafes
you? Recall once again the dilemma, 'if not a wise Providence, then a mere jumble of atoms', and consider the profu-
sion of evidence that this world is as it were a city. Do the
ills of the body afflict you? Reflect that the mind has but to
detach itself and apprehend its own powers, to be no longer
involved with the movements of the breath, whether they
be smooth or rough. In short, recollect all you have learnt
and accepted regarding pain and pleasure.

Or does the bubble reputation distract you? Keep before
your eyes the swift onset of oblivion, and the abysses of eternity before us and behind; mark how hollow are the echoes
of applause, how fickle and undiscerning the judgements of
professed admirers, and how puny the arena of human fame.
For the entire earth is but a point, and the place of our own
habitation but a minute corner in it; and how many are therein who will praise you, and what sort of men are they?

Remember then to withdraw into the little field of self.
Above all, never struggle or strain; but be master of yourself,
and view life as a man, as a human being, as a citizen, and
as a mortal. Among the truths you will do well to contemplate most frequently are these two: first, that things can
never touch the soul, but stand inert outside it, so that disquiet can arise only from fancies within; and secondly, that
all visible objects change in a moment, and will be no more.
Think of the countless changes in which you yourself have
had a part. The whole universe is change, and life itself is but
what you deem it.[1]

1. Life itself is but what you deem it. Hamlet (Act II, scene 2) says:
'There's nothing either good or bad but thinking makes it so.' Marcus

4. If the power of thought is universal among m[...]
likewise is the possession of reason, making[...]
creatures. It follows, therefore, that this reason speaks no less
universally to us all with its 'thou shalt' or 'thou shalt not'. So
then there is a world-law; which in turn means that we are
all fellow-citizens and share a common citizenship, and that
the world is a single city. Is there any other common citizenship that can be claimed by all humanity? And it is from
this world-polity that mind, reason, and law themselves
derive. If not, whence else? As the earthy portion of me has
its origin from earth, the watery from a different element,
my breath from one source and my hot and fiery parts from
another of their own elsewhere (for nothing comes from
nothing, or can return to nothing), so too there must be an
origin for the mind.

5. Death, like birth, is one of Nature's secrets; the same elements that have been combined are then dispersed. Nothing
about it need give cause for shame. For beings endowed with
mind it is no anomaly, nor in any way inconsistent with the
plan of their creation.

6. That men of a certain type should behave as they do is
inevitable. To wish it otherwise were to wish the fig-tree
would not yield its juice. In any case, remember that in a
very little while both you and he will be dead, and your very
names will quickly be forgotten.

7. Put from you the belief that 'I have been wronged', and
with it will go the feeling. Reject your sense of injury, and
the injury itself disappears.

8. What does not corrupt a man himself cannot corrupt his
life, nor do him any damage either outwardly or inwardly.

---

here expresses this thought more succinctly in two Greek words,
meaning literally 'life [is] opinion'.

9. The laws of collective expediency required this to happen.

10. Whatever happens, happens rightly. Watch closely, and you will find this true. In the succession of events there is not mere sequence alone, but an order that is just and right, as from the hand of one who dispenses to all their due. Keep up your watch, then, as you have begun, and let goodness accompany your every action – goodness, that is, in the proper sense of the word. In all your operations pay heed to this.

11. Do not copy the opinions of the arrogant, or let them dictate your own, but look at things in their true light.

12. At two points hold yourself always in readiness : first, to do exclusively what reason, our king and lawgiver, shall suggest for the common weal; and secondly, to reconsider a decision if anyone present should correct you and convince you of an error of judgement. But such conviction must proceed from the assurance that justice, or the common good, or some other such interest will be served. This must be the sole consideration; not the likelihood of pleasure or popularity.

13. Have you reason? 'I have.' Then why not use it? If reason does its part, what more would you ask?

14. As a part, you inhere in the Whole. You will vanish into that which gave you birth; or rather, you will be transmuted once more into the creative Reason of the universe.

15. Many grains of incense fall on the same altar : one sooner, another later – it makes no difference.

16. You have only to revert to the teachings of your creed, and to reverence for reason, and within a week those who now class you with beasts and monkeys will be calling you a god.

17. Live not as though there were a thousand years ahead of

you. Fate is at your elbow; make yourself good while life and power are still yours.

18. He who ignores what his neighbour is saying or doing or thinking, and cares only that his own actions should be just and godly, is greatly the gainer in time and ease. A good man does not spy around for the black spots in others, but presses unswervingly on towards his mark.

19. The man whose heart is palpitating for fame after death does not reflect that out of all those who remember him every one will himself soon be dead also, and in course of time the next generation after that, until in the end, after flaring and sinking by turns, the final spark of memory is quenched. Furthermore, even supposing that those who remember you were never to die at all, nor their memories to die either, yet what is that to you? Clearly, in your grave, nothing; and even in your lifetime, what is the good of praise – unless maybe to subserve some lesser design? Surely, then, you are making an inopportune rejection of what Nature has given you today, if all your mind is set on what men will say of you tomorrow.

20. Anything in any way beautiful derives its beauty from itself, and asks nothing beyond itself. Praise is no part of it, for nothing is made worse or better by praise. This applies even to the more mundane forms of beauty: natural objects, for example, or works of art. What need has true beauty of anything further? Surely none; any more than law, or truth, or kindness, or modesty. Is any of these embellished by praise, or spoiled by censure? Does the emerald lose its beauty for lack of admiration? Does gold, or ivory, or purple? A lyre or a dagger, a rosebud or a sapling?

21. If souls survive after death, how has the air above us found room for them all since time began? As well ask how

the earth finds room for all the bodies interred through im-memorial ages. There, after a short respite, change and decay make way for other dead bodies. Similarly, souls transferred to the air exist for a while before undergoing a change and a diffusion, and are then transmuted into fire and taken back into the creative principle of the universe; and thus room is made for the reception of others. Such will be the answer of any believer in the survival of souls. Moreover, we must reckon not only the number of human corpses so buried, but also that of all the creatures daily devoured by ourselves and the other animals. What multitudes, perishing in this way, are in a manner of speaking buried in the bodies of those whose nutriment they furnish! And yet, by their assi-milation into the blood and afterwards by the subsequent transmutation into the air or fire, all the needful space be-comes available.

How do we discover the truth of all this? By distinguishing between the matter and the cause.

22. Never allow yourself to be swept off your feet: when an impulse stirs, see first that it will meet the claims of justice; when an impression forms, assure yourself first of its certainty.

23. O world, I am in tune with every note of thy great har-mony. For me nothing is early, nothing late, if it be timely for thee. O Nature, all that thy seasons yield is fruit for me. From thee, and in thee, and to thee are all things. 'Dear city of God!' may we not cry, even as the poet cried 'Dear city of Cecrops!'[1]

---

1. Cecrops was the legendary founder of Athens, but the source of the quotation is unknown. In Marcus's noble phrase for the universe, 'dear city of God', St Augustine of Hippo found the title ready to his hand for his great Christian work, the *Civitas Dei*.

24. 'If thou wouldst know contentment, let thy deeds be few,' said the sage. Better still, limit them strictly to such as are essential, and to such as in a social being reason demands, and as it demands. This brings the contentment that comes of doing a few things and doing them well. Most of what we say and do is not necessary, and its omission would save both time and trouble. At every step, therefore, a man should ask himself, 'Is this one of the things that are superfluous?' More-over, not idle actions only but even idle impressions ought to be suppressed; for then unnecessary action will not ensue.

25. Test for yourself your capacity for the good man's life; the life of one content with his allotted part in the universe, who seeks only to be just in his doings and charitable in his ways.

26. You have seen all that?[1] – now look at this. Your part is to be serene, to be simple. Is someone doing wrong? The wrong lies with himself. Has something befallen you? Good; then it was your portion of the universal lot, assigned to you when time began; a strand woven into your particular web, like all else that happens. Life, in a word, is short; then snatch your profit from the passing hour, by obedience to reason and just dealing. Unbend, but be temperate.

27. Either a universe that is all order, or else a farrago thrown together at random yet somehow forming a universe. But can there be some measure of order subsisting in yourself, and at the same time disorder in the greater Whole? And that, too, when oneness of feeling exists between all the parts of nature, in spite of their divergence and dispersion?

28. A black heart![2] A womanish, wilful heart; the heart of

1. The unpleasant side of some recent encounter.
2. We can only guess at the reason for this uncharacteristic outburst. Had Marcus perhaps been re-reading a life of Nero?

a brute, a beast of the field; childish, stupid, and false; a huckster's heart, a tyrant's heart.

29. If he who knows not what is in the universe is a stranger to the universe, he is no less so who knows not what takes place in it. Such a man is an exile, self-banished from the polity of reason; a sightless man, having the eyes of his understanding darkened; a pauper dependent on others, without resources of his own for his livelihood. He is an excrescence on the world, when he dissociates and dissevers himself from the laws of our common nature by refusing to accept his lot (which after all is a product of the self-same Nature which produced yourself); he is a limb lopped from the community, when he cuts his own soul adrift from the single soul of all rational things.

30. One philosopher goes shirtless;[1] another bookless; a third, only half-clad, says, 'Bread have I none, yet still I cleave to reason.' For my part, I too have no fruit of my learning, and yet cleave to her.

31. Give your heart to the trade you have learnt, and draw refreshment from it. Let the rest of your days be spent as one who has whole-heartedly committed his all to the gods, and is thenceforth no man's master or slave.

32. Think, let us say, of the times of Vespasian;[2] and what

1. Many philosophers of the Cynic sect, holding that virtue was the sole object of life, contented themselves with the minimum of clothing and claimed that Nature was the only book a wise man need read. The Stoics regarded their own system as an offshoot from Cynicism; the Roman satirist Juvenal, in fact, jestingly asserts that you can only tell a Stoic from a Cynic because he wears a shirt (Satire xiii, 121).

2. The emperor Vespasian had died eighty-two years, and Trajan forty-four years, before Marcus ascended the throne.

do you see? Men and women busy marrying, bringing up children, sickening, dying, fighting, feasting, chaffering, farming, flattering, bragging, envying, scheming, calling down curses, grumbling at fate, loving, hoarding, coveting thrones and dignities. Of all that life, not a trace survives today. Or come forward to the days of Trajan; again, it is the same; that life, too, has perished. Take a similar look at the records of other past ages and peoples; mark how one and all, after their short-lived strivings, passed away and were resolved into the elements. More especially, recall some who, within your own knowledge, have followed after vanities instead of contenting themselves with a resolute performance of the duties for which they were created. In such cases it is essential to remind ourselves that the pursuit of any object depends for its value upon the worth of the object pursued. If, then, you would avoid discouragement, never become unduly absorbed in things that are not of the first importance.

33. Expressions that were once current have gone out of use nowadays. Names, too, that were formerly household words are virtually archaisms today; Camillus, Caeso, Volesus, Dentatus; or a little later, Scipio and Cato; Augustus too, and even Hadrian and Antoninus. All things fade into the storied past, and in a little while are shrouded in oblivion. Even to men whose lives were a blaze of glory this comes to pass; as for the rest, the breath is hardly out of them before, in Homer's words, they are 'lost to sight alike and hearsay'. What, after all, is immortal fame? An empty, hollow thing. To what, then, must we aspire? This, and this alone: the just thought, the unselfish act, the tongue that utters no falsehood, the temper that greets each passing event as something predestined, expected, and emanating from the One source and origin.

submit yourself to Clotho[1] with a good grace, and let her spin your thread out of what material she will.

35. All of us are creatures of a day; the rememberer and the remembered alike.

36. Observe how all things are continually being born of change; teach yourself to see that Nature's highest happiness lies in changing the things that are, and forming new things after their kind. Whatever is, is in some sense the seed of what is to emerge from it. Nothing can become a philosopher less than to imagine that seed can only be something that is planted in the earth or the womb.

37. Very soon you will be dead; but even yet you are not single-minded, nor above disquiet; not yet unapprehensive of harm from without; not yet charitable to all men, nor persuaded that to do justly is the only wisdom.

38. Observe carefully what guides the actions of the wise, and what they shun or seek.

39. For you, evil comes not from the mind of another; nor yet from any of the phases and changes of your own bodily frame. Then whence? From that part of yourself which acts as your assessor of what is evil. Refuse its assessment, and all is well. Though the poor body, so closely neighbouring it, be gashed or burned, fester or mortify, let the voice of this assessor remain silent; let it pronounce nothing to be bad or good if it can happen to evil men and good men alike – for anything that comes impartially upon men, whether they observe the rules of Nature or not, can neither be hindering her purposes nor advancing them.

1. Clotho, one of the three Fates, is she who spins the thread of men's lives; Lachesis decides their destiny; Atropos slits the thread when they must die.

40. Always think of the universe as one living organism, with a single substance and a single soul; and observe how all things are submitted to the single perceptivity of this one whole, all are moved by its single impulse, and all play their part in the causation of every event that happens. Remark the intricacy of the skein, the complexity of the web.

41. 'A poor soul burdened with a corpse,'[1] Epictetus calls you.

42. To be in process of change is not an evil, any more than to be the product of change is a good.

43. Time is a river, the resistless flow of all created things. One thing no sooner comes in sight than it is hurried past and another is borne along, only to be swept away in its turn.

44. Everything that happens is as normal and expected as the spring rose or the summer fruit; this is true of sickness, death, slander, intrigue, and all the other things that delight or trouble foolish men.

45. What follows is ever closely linked to what precedes; it is not a procession of isolated events, merely obeying the laws of sequence, but a rational continuity. Moreover, just as the things already in existence are all harmoniously coordinated, things in the act of coming into existence exhibit the same marvel of concatenation, rather than simply the bare fact of succession.

46. Always remember the dictum of Heraclitus, 'Death of earth, birth of water; death of water, birth of air; from air, fire; and so round again.' Remember also his 'wayfarer

1. The words do not occur in any of the surviving works of Epictetus, but suggested to Swinburne the line 'A little soul for a little bears up this corpse which is man' in his *Hymn to Proserpine*.

oblivious of where his road is leading', his 'men ever at odds with their own closest companion' (the controlling Reason of the universe), and his 'though they encounter this every day, they still deem it a stranger'. Again, 'we are not to act or speak like men asleep' (for indeed men in their sleep do fancy themselves to be acting and speaking), nor 'like children at their parents' word'; that is, in blind reliance on traditional maxims.

47. If a god were to tell you, 'Tomorrow, or at best the day after, you will be dead,' you would not, unless the most abject of men, be greatly solicitous whether it was to be the later day, rather than the morrow – for what is the difference between them? In the same way, do not reckon it of great moment whether it will come years and years hence, or tomorrow.

48. Remind yourself constantly of all the physicians, now dead, who used to knit their brows over their ailing patients; of all the astrologers who so solemnly predicted their clients' doom; the philosophers who expatiated so endlessly on death or immortality; the great commanders who slew their thousands; the despots who wielded powers of life and death with such terrible arrogance, as if themselves were gods who could never die; the whole cities which have perished completely, Helice, Pompeii, Herculaneum, and others without number. After that, recall one by one each of your own acquaintances; how one buried another, only to be laid low himself and buried in turn by a third, and all in so brief a space of time. Observe, in short, how transient and trivial is all mortal life; yesterday a drop of semen, tomorrow a handful of spice or ashes. Spend, therefore, these fleeting moments on earth as Nature would have you spend them, and then go to your rest with a good grace, as an olive falls in its season,

with a blessing for the earth that bore it and a thanksgiving
to the tree that gave it life.

49. Be like the headland against which the waves break and
break: it stands firm, until presently the watery tumult
around it subsides once more to rest. 'How unlucky I am,
that this should have happened to me!' By no means; say
rather, 'How lucky I am, that it has left me with no bitter-
ness; unshaken by the present, and undismayed by the future'
The thing could have happened to anyone, but not everyone
would have emerged unembittered. So why put the one down
to misfortune, rather than the other to good fortune? Can a
man call anything at all a misfortune, if it is not a contravention of his nature; and can it be a contravention of his
nature if it is not against that nature's will? Well, then: you
have learnt to know that will. Does this thing which has
happened hinder you from being just, magnanimous, temperate, judicious, discreet, truthful, self-respecting, independent,
and all else by which a man's nature comes to its fulfilment?
So here is a rule to remember in future, when anything
tempts you to feel bitter: not, 'This is a misfortune,' but 'To
bear this worthily is good fortune.'

50. Philosophy aside, an effectual help towards disregarding
death is to think of those who clung greedily to their lives.
What advantage have they over those who died young? In
every case, in some place at some time, the earth now covers
them all; Cadicianus, Fabius, Julianus, Lepidus, and the rest,
who saw so many to their graves, only to be seen to their own
at last. Brief, after all, was the respite they enjoyed; dragged
out in such conditions, and with such attendants, and in so
wretched a body. Set no store by it, then; look at the abyss of
time behind it, and the infinity yet to come. In the face of

75

that, what more is Nestor with all his years than any three-days babe?

51. Ever run the short way; and the short way is the way of nature, with perfect soundness in each word and deed as the goal. Such an aim will give you freedom from anxiety and strife, and from all compromise and artifice.

BOOK FIVE

1. At day's first light have in readiness, against disinclination to leave your bed, the thought that 'I am rising for the work of man'. Must I grumble at setting out to do what I was born for, and for the sake of which I have been brought into the world? Is this the purpose of my creation, to lie here under the blankets and keep myself warm? 'Ah, but it is a great deal more pleasant!' Was it for pleasure, then, that you were born, and not for work, not for effort? Look at the plants, the sparrows, ants, spiders, bees, all busy at their own tasks, each doing his part towards a coherent world-order; and will you refuse man's share of the work, instead of being prompt to carry out Nature's bidding? 'Yes, but one must have some repose as well.' Granted; but repose has its limits set by nature, in the same way as food and drink have; and you overstep these limits, you go beyond the point of sufficiency; while on the other hand, when action is in question, you stop short of what you could well achieve.

You have no real love for yourself; if you had, you would love your nature, and your nature's will. Craftsmen who love their trade will spend themselves to the utmost in labouring at it, even going unwashed and unfed; but you hold your nature in less regard than the engraver does his engraving, the dancer his dancing, the miser his heap of silver, or the vainglorious man his moment of glory. These men, when their heart is in it, are ready to sacrifice food and sleep to the advancement of their chosen pursuit. Is the service of the community of less worth in your eyes, and does it merit less devotion?

...he consolation of being able to thrust aside and cast into oblivion every tiresome intrusive impression, and in a trice be utterly at peace!

3. Reserve your right to any deed or utterance that accords with nature. Do not be put off by the criticisms or comments that may follow; if there is something good to be done or said, never renounce your right to it. Those who criticize you have their own reason to guide them, and their own impulse to prompt them; you must not let your eyes stray towards them, but keep a straight course and follow your own nature and the World-Nature (and the way of these two is one).

4. I travel the roads of nature until the hour when I shall lie down and be at rest; yielding back my last breath into the air from which I have drawn it daily, and sinking down upon the earth from which my father derived the seed, my mother the blood, and my nurse the milk of my being – the earth which for so many years has furnished my daily meat and drink, and, though so grievously abused, still suffers me to tread its surface.

5. You will never be remarkable for quick-wittedness. Be it so, then; yet there are still a host of other qualities whereof you cannot say, 'I have no bent for them.' Cultivate these, then, for they are wholly within your power : sincerity, for example, and dignity; industriousness, and sobriety. Avoid grumbling; be frugal, considerate, and frank; be temperate in manner and in speech; carry yourself with authority. See how many qualities there are which could be yours at this moment. You can allege no native incapacity or inaptitude for them; and yet you choose to linger still on a less lofty plane. Furthermore, is it any lack of natural endowments that necessitates those fits of querulousness and parsimony and fulsome flattery, of railing at your ill-health, of cringing and bragging

and continually veering from one mood to another? Most assuredly not; you could have rid yourself of all these long ago, and remained chargeable with nothing worse than a certain slowness and dulness of comprehension – and even this you can correct with practice, so long as you do not make light of it or take pleasure in your own obtuseness.

6. There is a type of person who, if he renders you a service, has no hesitation in claiming the credit for it. Another, though not prepared to go so far as that, will nevertheless secretly regard you as in his debt and be fully conscious of what he has done. But there is also the man who, one might almost say, has no consciousness at all of what he has done, like the vine which produces a cluster of grapes and then, having yielded its rightful fruit, looks for no more thanks than a horse that has run his race, a hound that has tracked his quarry, or a bee that has hived her honey. Like them, the man who has done one good action does not cry it aloud, but passes straight on to a second, as the vine passes on to the bearing of another summer's grapes.

'According to you, then, we should rank ourselves with things that act unconsciously?' Exactly; yet we should do so consciously; for, as the saying goes, 'awareness that his actions are social is the mark of a social being'. 'But also, surely, the wish that society itself should be equally aware of it?' True, no doubt; yet you miss the meaning of the aphorism, and so put yourself in the same class as the persons I have just described, who likewise are misled by a specious kind of reasoning. Apprehend the true significance of the saying, and you need never fear that it will betray you into omitting any social duty.

7. The Athenians pray, 'Rain, rain, dear Zeus, upon the fields

and plains of Athens.' Prayers should either not be offered at all, or else be as simple and ingenuous as this.

8. Just as we say, 'Aesculapius [1] has prescribed horseback exercise, or cold baths, or going barefoot,' so in the same way does the World-Nature prescribe disease, mutilation, loss, or some other disability. In the former case, prescribing meant ordering a specific treatment, in the interests of the patient's health; similarly in the latter, certain specific occurrences are ordered, in the interests of our destiny. We may, in fact, be said to 'meet with' these misfortunes in the same sense as masons say that the squared stones in walls or pyramids 'meet with' each other when they are being fitted closely together to make the unified whole. This mutual integration is a universal principle. As a myriad bodies combine into the single Body which is the world, so a myriad causes combine into the single Cause which is destiny. Even the common people realize this when they say, 'It was brought upon him.' It was indeed brought upon him; that is, it was prescribed for him. Let us accept such things, then, as we accept the prescriptions of an Aesculapius; for they, too, have often a harsh flavour, yet we swallow them gladly in hope of health. The execution and fulfilment of Nature's decrees should be viewed in the same way as we view our bodily health: even if what

1. By Aesculapius, Marcus here means any medical consultant. The original Aesculapius is mentioned by Homer merely as 'an excellent leech' who was the father of Machaon and Podalirius, the two physicians of the Greek army at Troy. In later times he appears with the rank of a divinity, presiding over the arts of healing and worshipped in his temples all over Greece. Serpents were everywhere associated with the cult of Aesculapius (the snake's periodic shedding of its skin causing it to be regarded as an apt symbol of renewed health and vigour); and the god's emblem of a serpent-wreathed staff was frequently placed by physicians at the head of their prescriptions. It is familiar today as the badge of the Royal Army Medical Corps.

befalls is unpalatable, nevertheless always receive it gladly, for it makes for the health of the universe, and even for the well-being and well-doing of Zeus himself. Had it not been for the benefit of the whole, he would never have brought it upon the individual. It is not Nature's way to bring anything upon that which is under her government, except what is specifically designed for its good. There are two reasons, then, why you should willingly accept what happens to you : first, because it happens to yourself, has been prescribed for yourself, and concerns yourself, being a strand in the tapestry of primordial causation; and secondly, because every individual dispensation is one of the causes of the prosperity, success, and even survival of That which administers the universe. To break off any particle, no matter how small, from the continuous concatenation – whether of causes or of any other elements – is to injure the whole. And each time you give way to discontent, you are causing, within your own limited ability, just such a breakage and disruption.

9. Do not be distressed, do not despond or give up in despair, if now and again practice falls short of precept. Return to the attack after each failure, and be thankful if on the whole you can acquit yourself in the majority of cases as a man should. But have a genuine liking for the discipline you return to ; do not recur to your philosophy in the spirit of a schoolboy to his master, but as the sore-eyed recur to their egg-and-sponge lotion, or as others to their poultice or their douche. In this way your submission to reason will not become a matter for public display, but for private consolation. Bear in mind that, while philosophy wills only what your own nature wills, you yourself were willing something else that was at variance with nature. 'Yes, but what other thing could have been more agreeable?' – is not that the inducement wherewith

pleasure seeks to beguile you? Yet consider: would not nobility of soul be more agreeable? Would not candour, simplicity, kindness, piety? Nay more; when you reflect on the precision and smoothness with which the processes of ratiocination and cognition operate, can there be anything more agreeable than the exercise of intellect?

10. As for truth, it is so veiled in obscurity that many reputable philosophers [1] assert the impossibility of reaching any certain knowledge. Even the Stoics admit that its attainment is beset with difficulties, and that all our intellectual conclusions are fallible; for where is the infallible man? Or turn from this to more material things: how transitory, how worthless are these – open to acquisition by every profligate, loose woman, and criminal. Or look at the characters of your own associates: even the most agreeable of them are difficult to put up with; and for the matter of that, it is difficult enough to put up with one's own self. In all this murk and mire, then, in all this ceaseless flow of being and time, of changes imposed and changes endured, I can think of nothing that is worth prizing highly or pursuing seriously. No; what a man must do is to nerve himself to wait quietly for his natural dissolution; and meanwhile not to chafe at its delay, but to find his sole consolation in two thoughts: first, that nothing can ever happen to us that is not in accordance with nature; and second, that power to abstain from acting against the divine spirit within me lies in my own hands, since there is no man alive who can force such disobedience upon me.

1. The reference is to the so-called 'Sceptic' or Pyrrhonian school of philosophers, founded by Pyrrho of Elis. They maintained that our perceptions can only show us things as they appear, and not as they are, and that a suspension of judgement is therefore the only correct attitude to anything.

11. To what use am I now putting the powers of my soul? Examine yourself on this point at every step, and ask, 'How stands it with that part of me men call the master-part? Whose soul inhabits me at this moment? A child's, a lad's, a woman's, a tyrant's, a dumb ox's, or a wild beast's?'

12. The popular conception of 'goods' can be tested in this way.[1] If the things a man identifies in his own mind with 'goods' are such things as prudence, temperance, justice, and fortitude, then, given that preconception, he will have no ears for the old jest about 'so many goods', for it will lack any point. On the other hand, if he shares the vulgar notion of what constitutes 'goods', he will readily appreciate the joker's quip, and have no difficulty in seeing its aptness. The majority do, in fact, entertain this idea of values, and they would never take offence at the witticism or refuse to hear it; indeed, we must accept it as an apt and clever observation if we take it to refer to wealth or things which conduce to luxury or prestige. So now for the test: ask yourself whether we do right to set store by things and think of them as 'goods', if our mental picture of them is such as to give meaning to the gibe that 'the owner of so many goods has no room left to ease himself'.

13. I consist of a formal element and a material. Neither of these can ever pass away into nothing, any more than either of them came into being from nothing. Consequently every part of me will one day be re-fashioned, by a process of transition,

1. This paragraph turns on the ambiguous meaning of the word 'goods'. The man in the street understands it to signify worldly possessions, rather than those virtues of character which are the true 'goods' in life. To a philosopher, on the other hand, the word would naturally convey this latter sense; and he would accordingly be puzzled by a reference to someone 'having so many goods that he has no room to relieve himself anywhere'.

into some other portion of the universe; which in its turn will again be changed into yet another part, and so onward to infinity. It is the same process by which I myself was brought into existence, and my parents before me, and so backward once more to infinity. (The phrase 'infinity' may pass, even if the world be in fact administered in finite cycles.)

14. Reason, and the act of reasoning, are self-sufficient faculties, both inherently and in the method of their operation. It is from sources in themselves that they acquire their initial impetus; and they travel straight forward to their own self-appointed goals. Actions of this kind accordingly receive the name of 'straightforwardness', in reference to the undeviating line they follow.

15. Unless things pertain to a man, as man, they cannot properly be said to belong to him. They cannot be required of him; for his nature neither promises them, nor is perfected by them. Therefore they cannot represent his chief end in life, nor even the 'good' which is the means to that end. Moreover, had man's natural heritage included such things, it could not at the same time have included contempt and renunciation of them; nor would the ability to do without them have been any cause for commendation; nor, supposing them to be really good, would failure to claim a full share of them be compatible with goodness. As it is, however, the more a man deprives himself, or submits to be deprived, of such things and their like, the more he grows in goodness.

16. Your mind will be like its habitual thoughts; for the soul becomes dyed with the colour of its thoughts. Soak it then in such trains of thought as, for example: Where life is possible at all, a right life is possible; life in a palace is possible; there-

fore even in a palace a right life is possible.[1] Or a
purpose behind each thing's creation determines its devel
ment; the development points to its final state; the final state
gives the clue to its chief advantage and good; therefore the
chief good of a rational being is fellowship with his neighbours – for it has been made clear long ago that fellowship
is the purpose behind our creation. (It is surely evident, is it
not, that while the lower exist for the higher, the higher
exist for one another? And while the animate is higher than
the inanimate, the rational is higher still.)

17. To pursue the unattainable is insanity, yet the thoughtless
can never refrain from doing so.

18. Nothing can happen to any man that nature has not fitted
him to endure. Your neighbour's experiences are no different
from your own; yet he, being either less aware of what has
happened or more eager to show his mettle, stands steady and
undaunted. For shame, that ignorance and vanity should
prove stronger than wisdom!

19. Outward things can touch the soul not a whit; they know
no way into it, they have no power to sway or move it. By
itself it sways and moves itself; it has its own self-approved
standards of judgement, and to them it refers every experience.

20. In one way humanity touches me very nearly, inasmuch
as I am bound to do good to my fellow-creatures and bear
with them. On the other hand, to the extent that individual
men hamper my proper activities, humanity becomes a thing
as indifferent to me as the sun, the wind, or the creatures of

1. Matthew Arnold found in these words the inspiration for his
sonnet beginning, ' "Even in a palace life may be lived well"; So
spake the imperial sage, purest of men, Marcus Aurelius.'

the wild. True, others may hinder the carrying out of certain actions; but they cannot obstruct my will, nor the disposition of my mind, since these will always safeguard themselves under reservations and adapt themselves to circumstances. The mind can circumvent all obstacles to action, and turn them to the furtherance of its main purpose, so that any impediment to its work becomes instead an auxiliary, and the barriers in its path become aids to progress.

21. In the universe, reverence that which is highest : namely, That to which all else ministers, and which gives the law to all. In like manner, too, reverence the highest in yourself: it is of one piece with the Other, since in yourself also it is that to which all the rest minister, and by which your life is directed.

22. What is not harmful to the city cannot harm the citizen. In every fancied case of harm, apply the rule, 'If the city is not harmed, I am not harmed either.' But if the city should indeed be harmed, never rage at the culprit : rather, find out at what point his vision failed him.

23. Reflect often upon the rapidity with which all existing things, or things coming into existence, sweep past us and are carried away. The great river of Being flows on without a pause; its actions for ever changing, its causes shifting endlessly, hardly a single thing standing still; while ever at hand looms infinity stretching behind and before – the abyss in which all things are lost to sight. In such conditions, surely a man were foolish to gasp and fume and fret, as though the time of his troubling could ever be of long continuance.

24. Think of the totality of all Being, and what a mite of it is yours; think of all Time, and the brief fleeting instant of it that is allotted to yourself; think of Destiny, and how puny a part of it you are.

25. Is one doing me wrong? Let himself look to that; his humours and his actions are his own. As for me, I am only receiving what the World-Nature wills me to receive, and acting as my own nature wills me to act.

26. Let no emotions of the flesh, be they of pain or pleasure, affect the supreme and sovereign portion of the soul. See that it never becomes involved with them; it must limit itself to its own domain, and keep the feelings confined to their proper sphere. If (through the sympathy which permeates any unified organism) they do spread to the mind, there need be no attempt to resist the physical sensation; only, the master-reason must refrain from adding its own assumptions of their goodness or badness.

27. Live with the gods. To live with the gods is to show them at all times a soul contented with their awards, and wholly fulfilling the will of that inward divinity, that particle of himself, which Zeus has given to every man for ruler and guide – the mind and the reason.

28. Do unsavoury armpits and bad breath make you angry? What good will it do you? Given the mouth and armpits the man has got, that condition is bound to produce those odours. 'After all, though, the fellow is endowed with reason, and he is perfectly able to understand what is offensive if he gives any thought to it.' Well and good: but you yourself are also endowed with reason; so apply your reasonableness to move him to a like reasonableness; expound, admonish. If he pays attention, you will have worked a cure, and there will be no need for passion; leave that to actors and streetwalkers.

29. It is possible to live on earth as you mean to live here-after. But if men will not let you, then quit the house of life; though not with any feeling of ill-usage. 'The hut smokes; I

move out.' No need to make a great business of it. Nevertheless, so long as nothing of the kind obliges me to depart, here I remain, my own master, and none shall hinder me from doing what I choose – and what I choose is to live the life that nature enjoins for a reasonable member of a social community.

30. The Mind of the universe is social. At all events, it has created the lower forms to serve the higher, and then linked together the higher in a mutual dependence on each other. Observe how some are subjected, others are connected, each and all are given their just due, and the more eminent among them are combined in mutual accord.

31. How have you behaved in the past to the gods, to your parents, your brothers, wife, children, teachers, tutors, friends, relatives, household? In all of these relationships, up to the present time, can you fairly echo the poet's line, 'Never a harsh word, never an injustice to a single person?' * Call to mind all you have passed through, and all you have been enabled to endure. Reflect that the story of your life is over, and your service at an end; bethink you of all the fair sights you have seen, the pleasures and the pains you have spurned, the many honours disdained, the many considerations shown to the inconsiderate.

32. How comes it that souls of no proficiency nor learning are able to confound the adept and the sage? Ah, but what soul is truly both adept and sage? His alone, who has knowledge of the beginning and the end, and of that all-pervading Reason which orders the universe in its determinate cycles to the end of time.

33. In a brief while now you will be ashes or bare bones; a

* Homer, *Odyssey*, iv, 690.

name, or perhaps not even a name – though even a name is no more than empty sound and reiteration. All that men set their hearts on in this life is vanity, corruption, and trash; men are like scuffling puppies, or quarrelsome children who are all smiles one moment and in tears the next. Faith and decency, justice and truth are fled 'up to Olympus from the wide-wayed earth'.* What is it, then, that still keeps you here? The objects of sense are mutable and transient, the organs of sense dim and easily misled, the poor soul itself a mere vapour exhaled from the blood,[1] and the world's praise, in such conditions, a vain thing. What then? Take heart, and wait for the end, be it extinction or translation. And what, think you, is all that is needful until that hour come? Why, what else but to revere and bless the gods; to do good to men; to bear and forbear; and to remember that whatsoever lies outside the bounds of this poor flesh and breath is none of yours, nor in your power.

34. Press on steadily, keep to the straight road in your thinking and doing, and your days will ever flow on smoothly. The soul of man, like the souls of all rational creatures, has two things in common with the soul of God : it can never be thwarted from without, and its good consists in righteousness of character and action, and in confining every wish thereto.

35. If the thing be no sin of mine, nor caused by any sin of mine, and if society be no worse for it, why give it further thought? How can it harm society?

36. Do not fall a too hasty prey to first impressions. Assist those in need, so far as you are able and they deserve it; but if their fall involves nothing morally significant, you must

---

1. According to the Stoic belief, the particle of divine fire which constitutes man's soul is nourished by the blood.

* Hesiod, *Works and Days*, v, 197.

not regard them as really injured, for that is not a good practice. Rather, in such cases be like the old fellow who pretended at his departure to beg eagerly for the slave-girl's top,[1] though knowing well that it was nothing more than a top.

When you are crying for votes on the platform, my friend, are you forgetting the ultimate worth of it all? 'I know; but these people set such store by it.' And does that justify you in sharing their folly?

No matter to what solitudes banished, I have always been a favourite of Fortune. For Fortune's favourite is the man who awards her good gifts to himself – the good gifts of a good disposition, good impulses, and good deeds.

1. The 'old fellow' made a kindly pretence of sharing the child's notion that its top was a precious and desirable treasure. In the same way, says Marcus, we should be sympathetic to the distress of others, even when our superior knowledge tells us that they have suffered no real harm.

BOOK SIX

1. Matter in the universe is supple and compliant, and the Reason which controls it has no motive for ill-doing; for it is without malice, and does nothing with intent to injure, neither is anything harmed by it. By its ordinances all things have their birth and their fulfilment.

2. If you are doing what is right, never mind whether you are freezing with cold or beside a good fire; heavy-eyed, or fresh from a sound sleep; reviled or applauded; in the act of dying, or about some other piece of business. (For even dying is part of the business of life; and there too no more is required of us than 'to see the moment's work well done'.)

3. Look beneath the surface: never let a thing's intrinsic quality or worth escape you.

4. All material objects swiftly change: either by sublimation (if the substance of the universe be indeed a unity), or else by dispersion.

5. Reason, the controller, has a perfect understanding of the conditions, the purpose, and the materials of its work.

6. To refrain from imitation is the best revenge.

7. Let your one delight and refreshment be to pass from one service to the community to another, with God ever in mind.

8. Our master-reason is something which is both self-awakened and self-directed. It cannot only make itself what it will, but also impose the aspect of its choice on anything which it experiences.

things come to their fulfilment as the one universal
_____ directs; for there is no rival nature, whether containing her from without, or itself contained within her, or even
existing apart and detached from her.

10. Either the world is a mere hotch-potch of random cohe-
sions and dispersions, or else it is a unity of order and providence. If the former, why wish to survive in such a purposeless and chaotic confusion; why care about anything, save the
manner of the ultimate return to dust; why trouble my head
at all; since, do what I will, dispersion must overtake me
sooner or later? But if the contrary be true, then I do reverence, I stand firmly, and I put my trust in the directing
Power.

11. When force of circumstance upsets your equanimity, lose
no time in recovering your self-control, and do not remain
out of tune longer than you can help. Habitual recurrence to
the harmony will increase your mastery of it.

12. If you had a stepmother at the same time as a mother,
you would do your duty by the former, but would still turn
continually to your mother. Here, you have both : the court
and philosophy. Time and again turn back to philosophy for
refreshment; then even the court life, and yourself in it, will
seem bearable.

13. When meat and other dainties are before you, you reflect:
This is dead fish, or fowl, or pig; or : This Falernian is some
of the juice from a bunch of grapes; my purple robe is sheep's
wool stained with a little gore from a shellfish; copulation is
friction of the members and an ejaculatory discharge. Reflections of this kind go to the bottom of things, penetrating into
them and exposing their real nature. The same process should
be applied to the whole of life. When a thing's credentials

look most plausible, lay it bare, observe its triviality, and strip it of the cloak of verbiage that dignifies it. Pretentiousness is the arch deceiver, and never more delusive than when you imagine your work is most meritorious. Note what Crates has to say about Xenocrates himself.[1]

14. The vulgar confine their admiration chiefly to things of an elementary order, which exist by virtue of mere inorganic cohesion or processes of nature; things of timber and stone, for example, or groves of figs and vines and olives. Minds of a somewhat higher degree of enlightenment are attracted by things that have animation, such as flocks and herds. A further step in refinement leads to admiration of the rational soul: rational, however, not yet in the sense of being part of the universal Reason, but simply as possessing certain skills in handicraft or other such talents – or even merely as owning large numbers of slaves. But the man who values a soul that is rational and universal and social no longer cares for anything else, but aims solely at keeping the temper of his own soul and all its activities rational and social, and works together with his fellows to this end.

15. One thing hastens into being, another hastens out of it. Even while a thing is in the act of coming into existence, some part of it has already ceased to be. Flux and change are for ever renewing the fabric of the universe, just as the ceaseless sweep of time is for ever renewing the face of eternity. In such a running river, where there is no firm foothold, what is there for a man to value among all the many things that are racing past him? It would be like setting the affections on some sparrow flitting by, which in the selfsame moment is lost to sight. A man's life is no more than an

1. The allusion is unknown.

inhalation from the air and an exhalation from the blood;[1] and there is no true difference between drawing in a single breath, only to emit it again, as we do every instant, and receiving the power to breathe at all, as you did but yesterday at your birth, only to yield it back one day to the source from which you drew it.

16. Transpiration is not a thing to be prized; we share it with the plants. Nor is respiration; we share that with the beasts of field and forest. Nor the perceptions of the senses, nor the twitchings of impulse, nor the instinct for gregariousness, nor the process of nutrition – which is in fact no more wonderful than that of excretion. So what, then, are we to value? The clapping of hands? No; and not the clapping of tongues either, which is all that the praise of the vulgar amounts to. Excluding then the delusions of fame, what is there left to be prized? In my judgement, this: to work out, in action and inaction alike, the purpose of our natural constitutions. That, after all, is the object of all training and all craftsmanship; for every craft aims at adapting a product to the end for which it was produced. The husbandman tending his vine, the groom breaking in his horse, the kennelman training his hound, all have this purpose in view. The labours of tutors and teachers, too, are directed to the same end. Here then is the prize we are looking for. Once make this truly your own, and no other objective will tempt you. Abandon all the other ambitions you cherish, or else you will never be your own master, never be independent of others or proof against passion. You will be bound to look with envy, jealousy, and suspicion at anyone who might rob you of those things, and to intrigue against anyone who happens to possess the treasure you covet for yourself. The belief that

1. See page 89, note 1.

things of that kind are indispensable is sure to
moil within, and too often leads on to murm
the gods as well; whereas a respect and esteem
understanding will keep you at peace with yourself, at one
with mankind, and in harmony with the gods; gladly
acquiescent, that is, with whatever they dispense or ordain.

17. Above, below, and around us whirl the elements in their
courses. But virtue knows no such motions: she is a thing
more divine, moving serenely onward in ways past understanding.

18. How strange are the ways of men! They will spare no
word of praise for their contemporaries, who live in their very
midst, and yet they covet greatly for themselves the praise of
future generations, whom they have never seen and never
will see. Almost as well grumble at not having praise from
one's ancestors!

19. Because a thing is difficult for you, do not therefore suppose it to be beyond mortal power. On the contrary, if anything is possible and proper for man to do, assume that it
must fall within your own capacity.

20. When an opponent in the gymnasium gashes us with his
nails or bruises our head in a collision, we do not protest or
take offence, and we do not suspect him ever afterwards of
malicious intent. However, we do regard him with a wary
eye; not in enmity or suspicion, yet good-temperedly keeping
our distance. So let it be, too, at other times in life; let us
agree to overlook a great many things in those who are, as it
were, our fellow-contestants. A simple avoidance, as I have
said, is always open to us, without either suspicion or ill-
will.

21. If anyone can show me, and prove to me, that I am wrong in thought or deed, I will gladly change. I seek the truth, which never yet hurt anybody. It is only persistence in self-delusion and ignorance which does harm.

22. I do that which it is my duty to do. Nothing else distracts me; for it will be either something that is inanimate and irrational, or somebody who is misled and ignorant of the way.

23. Be generous and liberal in your attitude to irrational creatures and to the generality of material things, for you have reason and they have none. Human beings, on the other hand, have reason; so treat them in a spirit of fellowship. In all things call upon the gods for help – yet without too many scruples about the length of your prayers; three hours so spent will suffice.

24. In death, Alexander of Macedon's end differed no whit from his stable-boy's. Either both were received into the same generative principle of the universe, or both alike were dispersed into atoms.

25. Think of the number of things, bodily and mental, that are going on at the same moment within each one of us; and then it will not surprise you that an infinitely greater number of things – everything, in fact, that comes to birth in this vast One-and-All we call the universe – can exist simultaneously therein.

26. If you were asked to spell the name Antoninus, would you rap out each letter at the top of your voice, and then, if your hearers grew angry, grow angry yourself in turn? Rather, would you not proceed to enumerate the several letters quietly one by one? Well then; remember that here in life

every piece of duty is likewise made up of its separate items. Pay careful attention to each of these, without fuss and without returning temper for temper, and so ensure the methodical completion of your appointed task.

27. How barbarous, to deny men the privilege of pursuing what they imagine to be their proper concerns and interests! Yet, in a sense, this is just what you are doing when you allow your indignation to rise at their wrongdoing; for after all, they are only following their own apparent concerns and interests. You say they are mistaken? Why then, tell them so, and explain it to them, instead of being indignant.

28. Death: a release from impressions of sense, from twitchings of appetite, from excursions of thought, and from service to the flesh.

29. Shame on the soul, to falter on the road of life while the body still perseveres.

30. Be careful not to affect the monarch too much, or to be too deeply dyed with the purple; for this can well happen. Keep yourself simple, good, pure, serious, and unassuming; the friend of justice and godliness; kindly, affectionate, and resolute in your devotion to duty. Strive your hardest to be always such a man as Philosophy would have you to be. Reverence the gods, succour your fellow-mortals. Life is short, and this earthly existence has but a single fruit to yield – holiness within, and selfless action without. Be in all things Antoninus's disciple; remember his insistence on the control of conduct by reason, his calm composure on all occasions, and his own holiness; the serenity of his look and the sweetness of his manner; his scorn of notoriety, and his zeal for the mastery of facts; how he would never dismiss a subject until he had looked thoroughly into it and understood it clearly;

how he would suffer unjust criticisms without replying in kind; how he was never hasty, and no friend to tale-bearers; shrewd in his judgements of men and manners, yet never censorious; wholly free from nervousness, suspicion, and over-subtlety; how easily satisfied he was in such matters as lodging, bed, dress, meals, and service; how industrious, and how patient; how, thanks to his frugal diet, he could remain at work from morning till night without even attending to the calls of nature until his customary hour; how firm and constant he was in his friendships, tolerating the most outspoken opposition to his own opinions, and welcoming any suggested amendments; what reverence, untainted by the smallest trace of superstition, he showed to the gods. Remember all this, so that when your own last hour comes your conscience may be as clear as his.

31. Come back now to your sober senses; recall your true self; awake from slumber, and recognize that they were only dreams that troubled you; and as you looked on them, so look now on what meets your waking eyes.

32. A body and a soul comprise myself. To the body all things are indifferent, for it is incapable of making distinctions. To the mind, the only things not indifferent are its own activities, and these are all under its control. Even with them, moreover, its sole concern is with those of the present moment; once they are past, or when they still lie in the future, they themselves at once come to be indifferent.

33. Pain of hand or foot is nothing unnatural, so long as hand and foot are doing their own work. Likewise no pain is contrary to the nature of man, as man, so long as he is doing man's work. And if it accords with nature, it cannot be an evil.

34. In what extraordinary pleasures do robbers, perverts, parricides, and tyrants find their enjoyment!

35. Notice how common artificers will meet the wishes of an unskilled employer up to a certain point, but none the less stand fast by the rules of their trade and refuse to depart from them. Is it not deplorable that a builder or a physician should have more respect for the canons of his craft than man has for his own, which he shares with the gods?

36. In the universe Asia and Europe are but two small corners, all ocean's waters a drop, Athos a puny lump of earth, the vastness of time a pin's point in eternity. All is petty, inconstant, and perishable. All proceeds from the one source, springing either directly or derivatively from the universal sovereign Reason. Even the lion's open jaws, the deadly poison, and all other things that do hurt, down to the bramble-bush and the slough, are by-products of something else that is itself noble and beautiful. Do not think of them, then, as alien to That which you reverence, but remember the one origin that is common to them all.

37. To see the things of the present moment is to see all that is now, all that has been since time began, and all that shall be unto the world's end; for all things are of one kind and one form.

38. Think often of the bond that unites all things in the universe, and their dependence upon one another. All are, as it were, interwoven, and in consequence linked in mutual affection; because their orderly succession is brought about by the operation of the currents of tension,[1] and the unity of all substance.

1. An explanation of the Stoic theory of 'tension' is given in the Introduction, page 14.

39. Adapt yourself to the environment in which your lot has been cast, and show true love to the fellow-mortals with whom destiny has surrounded you.

40. All is well with a tool, instrument, or utensil when it serves the use for which it was made, though in this case its maker is not present. But with things formed by Nature, the power that fashioned them is still within them, and remains in them. All the more, then, should you have it in reverence, and be assured that if only you live and act according to its will, you have all things to your liking. That is the way in which the universe, too, has all things to its liking.

41. If you suppose anything over which you have no control to be either good or bad for you, then the accident of missing the one or encountering the other is certain to make you aggrieved with the gods, and bitter against the men whom you know or suspect to be responsible for your failure or misfortune. We do, in fact, commit many injustices through attaching importance to things of this class. But when we limit our notions of good and evil strictly to what is within our own power, there remains no reason either to bring accusations against God or to set ourselves at variance with men.

42. All of us are working together for the same end; some of us knowingly and purposefully, others unconsciously (as Heraclitus, I think, has remarked that 'even in their sleep men are at work' and contributing their share to the cosmic process). To one man falls this share of the task, to another that; indeed, no small part is performed by that very malcontent who does all he can to hinder and undo the course of events. The universe has need even of such as he. It remains for you, then, to consider with whom you will range yourself; for in any case he who directs all things will find

some good use to make of you, and give you your place among his helpmates and fellow-labourers. Only, have a care that yours is not that sorry function which, according to Chrysippus, is performed by the clown's part on the stage.[1]

43. Does the sun think to do the rain's work? Or Asclepius that of Demeter? And how is it with the stars? Are they not all different, yet all work in concert to the one end?

44. If the gods took counsel together about myself, and what should befall me, then their counsel was good. For it were hard to conceive of divinity counselling unwisely. After all, what incentive would they have to work my hurt? Where would be the gain, either to themselves, or to the universe which is their chief care? Even if they took no special thought for myself, at least they took thought for the universe; and I ought to welcome and feel kindly disposed towards anything that happens as a result. If, of course, they took no thought for anything at all – an impious thing to believe – why then, let us make an end of sacrifice and prayer and vow, and all other actions whereby we acknowledge the presence of living gods in our midst. Yet even so, and even if it is true that they care nothing for our mortal concerns, I am still able to take care of myself and to look to my own interests; and the interest of every creature lies in conformity with its own constitution and nature. My own nature is a rational and civic one; I have a city, and I have a country; as Marcus I have Rome, and as a human being I have the universe; and consequently, what is beneficial to these communities is the sole good for me.

45. All that befalls the individual is for the good of the whole. That by itself is warrant enough for us; but if you look closely

1. i.e. to provide that element of baseness against which nobility shows up more clearly.

you will also notice that, as a general rule, what is good for one man is good for his fellow-men as well. ('Good', though, must be taken here in the more popular sense, as inclusive of things that are morally indifferent.)

46. As the performances in the circus or in other places of entertainment tire one with their perpetual repetition of the same sights, the monotony of which makes the spectacle a weariness, so it is with the whole experience of life: on our upward and downward path all things prove to be ever the same – causes and effects alike. How long then … ?

47. Often ponder in your mind the multitudes of the dead of every calling and nation, down even to Philistion and Phoebus and Origanion.[1] From these latest, let your thoughts pass to the hosts of others; think how we must follow whither so many great orators are gone before, so many reverend sages – Heraclitus, Pythagoras, Socrates – the heroes of early days, the captains and the kings of after-ages, and with them Eudoxus, Hipparchus, Archimedes, and many another; keen wits, sublime spirits, men unwearied, resourceful, and resolute; those too who made a merry jest of the transience and brevity of this mortal life in the fashion of Menippus and his school. Muse often on these men, all long since laid low in death. How, pray, are they the worse for it now – more especially those whose very names have been forgotten? In this life one thing only is of precious worth: to live out one's

1. Philistion, Phoebus, and Origanion are unknown to us; the language suggests that they are persons who had died recently. Eudoxus is said to have been learned in astrology, medicine, and law. Hipparchus was a mathematician of note. The scientific reputation of Archimedes survives to this day. Of the Greek philosopher Menippus, Diogenes Laertius remarks that 'he published nothing memorable, but his writings abound in humour and laughter' (vi, 99).

days in truthfulness and fair dealing, and in
with the false and unjust.

48. When you would have a cordial for your spirits, think of
the good qualities of your friends: this one's capability, that
one's self-effacement, another's generosity, and so forth.
There is no surer remedy for dejection than to see examples
of the different virtues displayed in the characters of those
around us, exhibiting themselves as plenteously as can be.
Wherefore keep them ever before you.

49. Do you make a grievance of weighing so many pounds
only, instead of three hundred? Then why fret about living
so many years only, instead of more? Since you are content
with the measure of substance allowed you, be so also with
the measure of time.

50. Try to move men by persuasion; yet act against their will
if the principles of justice so direct. But if someone uses force
to obstruct you, then take a different line; resign yourself
without a pang, and turn the obstacle into an opportunity
for the exercise of some other virtue. Your attempt was always
subject to reservations, remember; you were not aiming at the
impossible. At what, then? Simply at making the attempt
itself. In this you succeeded; and with that, the object of your
existence is attained.

51. The man of ambition thinks to find his good in the
operations of others; the man of pleasure in his own sensations; but the man of understanding in his own actions.

52. You are not compelled to form any opinion about this
matter before you, nor to disturb your peace of mind at all.
Things in themselves have no power to extort a verdict from
you.

53. Accustom yourself to give careful attention to what others are saying, and try your best to enter into the mind of the speaker.

54. What is no good for the hive is no good for the bee.

55. If the crew took to vilifying their steersman, or the patients their doctor, is there any other they would listen to instead; and how would such another be able to ensure the safety of the sailors, or the health of the sick?

56. How many who came into this world with me have already left it!

57. To a man with jaundice, honey seems bitter; to one bitten by a mad dog, water is a thing of horror; to little children, a ball is a treasure of great price. Why then do I give way to anger? For can it be supposed that a man's erroneous thinking has any less effect on him than the bile in jaundice, or the virus in hydrophobia?

58. No one can stop you living according to the laws of your own personal nature, and nothing can happen to you against the laws of the World-Nature.

59. What sorry creatures are the men folk seek to please! What sorry ends they pursue, and by what sorry means! How quickly time shall cover all things! How many has it covered even now!

BOOK SEVEN

1. What is evil? A thing you have seen times out of number. Likewise with every other sort of occurrence also, be prompt to remind yourself that this, too, you have witnessed many times before. For everywhere, above and below, you will find nothing but the selfsame things; they fill the pages of all history, ancient, modern, and contemporary; and they fill our cities and homes today. There is no such thing as novelty; all is as trite as it is transitory.

2. Principles can only lose their vitality when the first impressions from which they derive have sunk into extinction; and it is for you to keep fanning these continually into fresh flame. I am well able to form the right impression of a thing; and given this ability, there is no need to disquiet myself. (As for things that are beyond my understanding, they are no concern of my understanding.) Once learn this, and you stand erect. A new life lies within your grasp. You have only to see things once more in the light of your first and earlier vision, and life begins anew.

3. An empty pageant; a stage play; flocks of sheep, herds of cattle; a tussle of spearmen; a bone flung among a pack of curs; a crumb tossed into a pond of fish; ants, loaded and labouring; mice, scared and scampering; puppets, jerking on their strings – that is life. In the midst of it all you must take your stand, good-temperedly and without disdain, yet always aware that a man's worth is no greater than the worth of his ambitions.

4. In talk, mark carefully what is being said, and when action is afoot, what is being done. In the latter case, look at once

...at is purposed; and in the other, make certain what
... ...

5. Is my understanding equal to this task, or not? If it is, I apply it to the work as a tool presented to me by Nature. If not, then either I make way – if my duty permits it – for someone more capable of doing the business, or else I do the best I can with the help of some assistant, who will avail himself of my inspiration to achieve what is timely and serviceable for the community. For everything I do, whether by myself or with another, must have as its sole aim the service and harmony of all.

6. How many whose praises used once to be sung so loudly are now relegated to oblivion; and how many of the singers themselves have long since passed from our sight!

7. Think it no shame to be helped. Your business is to do your appointed duty, like a soldier in the breach. How, then, if you are lame, and unable to scale the battlements yourself, but could do it if you had the aid of a comrade?

8. Never let the future disturb you. You will meet it, if you have to, with the same weapons of reason which today arm you against the present.

9. All things are interwoven with one another; a sacred bond unites them; there is scarcely one thing that is isolated from another. Everything is coordinated, everything works together in giving form to the one universe. The world-order is a unity made up of multiplicity: God is one, pervading all things; all being is one, all law is one (namely, the common reason which all thinking creatures possess) and all truth is one – if, as we believe, there can be but one path to perfection for beings that are alike in kind and reason.

10. Swiftly each particle of matter vanishes into the universal Substance; swiftly each item of causation is reassumed into the universal Reason; swiftly the remembrance of all things is buried in the gulf of eternity.

11. To a reasoning being, an act that accords with nature is an act that accords with reason.

12. To stand up – or be set up?

13. In a system comprising diverse elements, those which possess reason have the same part to play as the bodily limbs in an organism that is a unity; being similarly constituted for mutual cooperation. This reflection will impress you more forcibly if you constantly tell yourself, 'I am a "limb" (*melos*) of the whole complex of rational things.' If you think of yourself as a 'part' (*meros*) only, you have as yet no love from the heart for mankind, and no joy in the performance of acts of kindness for their own sake. You do them as a bare duty, and not yet as good offices to yourself.

14. Come what will upon such parts of me as can be affected by its incidence; they may complain of it if they will. As for myself, if I do not view the thing as an evil, I take no hurt. And nothing compels me to view it so.

15. Whatever the world may say or do, my part is to keep myself good; just as a gold piece, or an emerald, or a purple robe insists perpetually, 'Whatever the world may say or do, my part is to remain an emerald and keep my colour true.'

16. The master-reason is never the victim of any self-disturbance; it never, for example, excites passions within itself. If another can inspire it with terror or pain, let him do so; but by itself it never permits its own assumptions to mislead it into such moods. By all means let the body take thought for

itself to avoid hurt, if it can; and if it be hurt, let it say so. But the soul, which alone can know fear or pain, and on whose judgement their existence depends, takes no harm; you cannot force the verdict from it. The master-reason is self-sufficient, knowing no needs except those it creates for itself, and by the same token can experience no disturbances or obstructions unless they be of its own making.

17. Happiness, by derivation, means 'a good god within';[1] that is, a good master-reason. Then what, vain Fancy, are *you* doing here? Be off, in heaven's name, as you came; I want none of you. I know it is long habit that brings you here, and I bear no ill-will; but get you gone.

18. We shrink from change; yet is there anything that can come into being without it? What does Nature hold dearer, or more proper to herself? Could you have a hot bath unless the firewood underwent some change? Could you be nourished if the food suffered no change? Is it possible for any useful thing to be achieved without change? Do you not see, then, that change in yourself is of the same order, and no less necessary to Nature?

19. All bodies pass through the universal substance, as it were into and out of a rushing stream; cohering and co-operating with the whole, as do our physical members with one another. How many a Chrysippus, a Socrates, an Epictetus has been engulfed by time! Remember this when you have to do with any man or thing whatsoever.

20. One thing alone troubles me: the fear that I may do something which man's constitution disallows, or would wish to be done in some other way, or forbids till a future day.

1. This is the meaning of *eudaimonia*, the Greek word for happiness.

21. Soon you will have forgotten the world, and world will have forgotten you.

22. It is man's peculiar distinction to love even those who err and go astray. Such a love is born as soon as you realize that they are your brothers; that they are stumbling in ignorance, and not wilfully; that in a short while both of you will be no more; and, above all, that you yourself have taken no hurt, for your master-reason has not been made a jot worse than it was before.

23. Out of the universal substance, as out of wax, Nature fashions a colt, then breaks him up and uses the material to form a tree, and after that a man, and next some other thing; and not one of these endures for more than a brief span. As for the vessel itself, it is no greater hardship to be taken to pieces than to be put together.

24. An angry look on the face is wholly against nature. If it be assumed frequently, beauty begins to perish, and in the end is quenched beyond rekindling. You must try to realize that this shows the unreasonableness of it; for if we lose the ability to perceive our faults, what is the good of living on?

25. Only a little while, and Nature, the universal disposer, will change everything you see, and out of their substance will make fresh things, and yet again others from theirs, to the perpetual renewing of the world's youthfulness.

26. When anyone offends against you, let your first thought be, Under what conception of good and ill was this committed? Once you know that, astonishment and anger will give place to pity. For either your own ideas of what is good are no more advanced than his, or at least bear some likeness to them, in which case it is clearly your duty to pardon him;

or else, on the other hand, you have grown beyond supposing such actions to be either good or bad, and therefore it will be so much the easier to be tolerant of another's blindness.

27. Do not indulge in dreams of having what you have not, but reckon up the chief of the blessings you do possess, and then thankfully remember how you would crave for them if they were not yours. At the same time, however, beware lest delight in them leads you to cherish them so dearly that their loss would destroy your peace of mind.

28. Withdraw into yourself. Our master-reason asks no more than to act justly, and thereby to achieve calm.

29. Do away with all fancies. Cease to be passion's puppet. Limit time to the present. Learn to recognize every experience for what it is, whether it be your own or another's. Divide and classify the objects of sense into cause and matter. Meditate upon your last hour. Leave your neighbour's wrong-doing to rest with him who initiated it.

30. Fix your thought closely on what is being said, and let your mind enter fully into what is being done, and into what is doing it.

31. Put on the shining face of simplicity and self-respect, and of indifference to everything outside the realms of virtue or vice. Love mankind. Walk in God's ways. 'All under law,' quoth the sage; and what though his saying had reference to atoms alone? For us, it suffices to remember that all things are indeed under law. Three words, but enough.

32. Of Death. Dispersion, if the world be a concourse of atoms: extinction or transmutation, if it be a unity.

33. Of Pain. If it is past bearing, it makes an end of us; if it lasts, it can be borne. The mind, holding itself aloof from the

body, retains its calm, and the master-reason remains un-affected. As for the parts injured by the pain, let them, if they can, declare their own grief.

34. Of Fame. Take a look at the minds of her suitors, their ambitions and their aversions. Furthermore, reflect how speedily in this life the things of today are buried under those of tomorrow, even as one layer of drifting sand is quickly covered by the next.

35. 'If a man has greatness of mind, and the breadth of vision to contemplate all time and all reality, can he regard human life as a thing of any great consequence?' – 'No, he cannot.' – 'So he won't think death anything to be afraid of?' – 'No.' (From Plato.*)

36. 'It is the fate of princes to be ill spoken of for well-doing.' (From Antisthenes.)

37. It is a shame for the features to order and dispose them-selves obediently as the mind directs, while the same mind refuses to order and dispose itself.

38. 'Vex not thy spirit at the course of things;
    They heed not thy vexation.' †

39. 'To the deathless gods and likewise to ourselves give joy.'‡

40. 'Like ears of corn the lives of men are reaped;
    This one is left to stand, and that cut down.'§

41. 'If Heav'n care nought for me and my two boys,
    There must be some good reason even for this.' ‖

42. 'Right and good fortune both are on my side.' ¶

---

* *Republic*, 486.   † Euripides, *Bellerophon*, Frag. 289.
‡ Source unknown.   § Euripides, *Hypsipyle*, Frag. 757.
‖ Euripides, *Antiope*, Frag. 207.   ¶ Euripides, Frag. 910.

43. 'No tears with those who wail, no quickening of the pulse.'*

44. 'I might fairly reply to him, You are mistaken, my friend, if you think that a man who is worth anything ought to spend his time weighing up the prospects of life and death. He has only one thing to consider in performing any action : that is, whether he is acting rightly or wrongly, like a good man or a bad one.' (From Plato.†)

45. 'The truth of the matter is this, gentlemen. When a man has once taken up his stand, either because it seems best to him or in obedience to orders, there I believe he is bound to remain and face the danger, taking no account of death or anything else before dishonour.' (From Plato.‡)

46. 'But I beg you, my friend, to think it possible that nobility and goodness may be something different from keeping one-self and one's friends from danger, and to consider whether a true man, instead of clinging to life at all costs, ought not to dismiss from his mind the question how long he may have to live. Let him leave that to the will of God, in the belief that the womenfolk are right when they tell us that no man can escape his destiny, and let him devote himself to the next problem, how he can best live the life allotted to him.' (From Plato.§)

47. Survey the circling stars, as though yourself were in mid-course with them. Often picture the changing and re-changing dance of the elements. Visions of this kind purge away the dross of our earth-bound life.

48. Plato has a fine saying, that he who would discourse of man should survey, as from some high watchtower, the

---

* Source unknown.   † *Apology*, 28 B.
‡ *Apology*, 28 E.   § *Gorgias*, 512 DE.

things of earth; its assemblies for peace or war, its husbandry, matings, and partings, births and deaths, noisy law-courts, lonely wastes, alien peoples of every kind, feasting, mourning, bargaining – observing all the motley mixture, and the harmonious order that is wrought out of contrariety.

49. Look back over the past, with its changing empires that rose and fell, and you can foresee the future too. Its pattern will be the same, down to the last detail; for it cannot break step with the steady march of creation. To view the lives of men for forty years or forty thousand is therefore all one; for what more will there be for you to see?

50. 'All born of earth must unto earth return;
     All growths of heav'nly seed to heav'n revert.' *
– by the disintegration, that is, of their atomic structure and the dispersion of their uncaring elements.

51. 'What, turn aside with meats and drinks and charms
     The tides of Destiny, and so 'scape Death?'†

    'The gales that blow from God must needs be faced
     With labouring oars and uncomplaining hearts.' ‡

52. 'More crafty in the ring,' [1] no doubt – but not more public-spirited, more self-effacing, more disciplined to circumstance, more indulgent to a neighbour's oversights.

53. If a deed can be accomplished to accord with that reason which men share with gods, there is nothing to fear. Where

---

1. In the Greek, literally 'a better thrower-down'. The word occurs in one of Plutarch's anecdotes, where a crestfallen Spartan wrestler complains that his victorious opponent was 'not any brainier, not any brawnier, merely a better thrower-down'. The story seems to have put Marcus in mind of some contemporary political figure.

* Euripides, *Chrysippus*, Frag. 836.

† Euripides, *Suppliants*, 1110.   ‡ Source unknown.

service presents itself, by some action that will go
rward in obedience to the laws of our being, we
r no harm.

54. In your power at all times and places there lies a pious
acceptance of the day's happenings, a just dealing towards the
day's associates, and a scrupulous attention to the day's impressions, lest any of them gain an entrance unverified.

55. Cast no side-glance at the instincts governing other men,
but keep your eyes fixed on the goal whereto nature herself
guides you – the World-Nature speaking through circumstance, and your own nature speaking through the calls of
duty. The acts of man should accord with his natural constitution; and while all other created things are constituted
for the service of rational beings (in accordance with the
general law by which the lower exists for the good of the
higher), these latter are constituted to serve one another. Chief
of all features in a man's constitution, therefore, is his duty to
his kind. Next after that comes his obligation to resist the
murmurs of the flesh; for it is the particular office of his reason
and intellect to maintain such a fence around their own
workings that they are not overborne by those of the senses
or the impulses, both of which are animal in quality. Mind
demands the premier place, and will not bow to their yoke;
and rightly so, since nature has formed it to make use of all
the rest. And thirdly, the constitution of a rational being
should make him incapable of indiscretion, and proof against
imposture. Let but Reason, the helmsman, steer a straight
course, holding fast by these three principles, and be sure
it will come by its own.

56. Take it that you have died today, and your life's story is
ended; and henceforward regard what further time may be

given you as an uncovenanted surplus, and live it out in ⌉
harmony with nature.

57. Love nothing but that which comes to you woven in the
pattern of your destiny. For what could more aptly fit your
needs?

58. In any predicament, have before your eyes the case of
other men who greeted a like crisis with indignation, astonishment, and outcry. Where are they now? Nowhere. Then
why wish to follow their example? Rather, leave another's
humours to their own master or servant, and give all your
attention to turning the event itself to some good account.
In this way you will be making the best use of it, and it will
serve you as working material. In every action let your own
self-approval be the sole aim both of your effort and of your
intention; bearing in mind that the event itself which
prompted your action is a thing of no consequence to either
of them.

59. Dig within. There lies the well-spring of good: ever dig,
and it will ever flow.

60. Also let your bodily carriage be firm, and without con-
tortions, whether in motion or at rest. As the mind reveals
itself in the face, by keeping the features composed and
decent, so the same should be required of it in respect of the
whole body. All this, however, must be ensured without any
sort of affectation.

61. The art of living is more like wrestling than dancing,
in as much as it, too, demands a firm and watchful stance
against any unexpected onset.

62. Always get to know the characters of those whose

approval you wish to earn, and the nature of their guiding principles. Look into the sources of their opinions and their motives, and then you will not blame any of their involuntary offences, or feel the want of their approbation.

63. 'No soul', it has been said, 'forfeits truth wilfully.' * And the same holds good for justice, self-control, kindliness, or any other virtue. Nothing needs to be kept in mind more constantly than this; it will help you to greater gentleness in all your dealings with people.

64. When in pain, always be prompt to remind yourself that there is nothing shameful about it and nothing prejudicial to the mind at the helm, which suffers no injury either in its rational or its social aspect. In most cases the saying of Epicurus should prove helpful, that 'Pain is never unbearable or unending, so long as you remember its limitations and do not indulge in fanciful exaggerations.' Bear in mind also that, though we do not realize it, many other things which we find uncomfortable are, in fact, of the same nature as pain : feelings of lethargy, for example, or a feverish temperature, or loss of appetite. When inclined to grumble at any of these, tell yourself that you are giving in to pain.

65. When men are inhuman, take care not to feel towards them as they do towards other humans.

66. How do we know that Telauges [1] may not have been a better man than Socrates? It is all very well to argue that Socrates died a finer death, or disputed more acutely with the sophists, or stood up more hardily to the rigours of a frosty night; that he spiritedly resisted the order to arrest

1. The son of Pythagoras, and according to some the teacher of Empedocles (Diogenes Laertius, viii, 43).

* Plato, quoted by Epictetus (i, xxviii, 4).

Leon of Salamis,[1] or 'stalked the streets in majesty'[2] (though the truth of this last may well be questioned) – but the real point to consider is, What kind of a soul did he have? Did he ask nothing more than to be found just towards men and pure before the gods? Did he avoid either resentment at the vices of others or submission to their ignorance? Did he accept what destiny assigned to him, not looking on it as something unnatural, nor suffering it as an unbearable affliction, nor allowing his mind to be influenced by the experiences of the flesh?

67. Nature has not blended mind so inextricably with body as to prevent it from establishing its own frontiers and controlling its own domain. It is perfectly possible to be godlike, even though unrecognized as such. Always keep that in mind; and also remember that the needs of a happy life are very few. Mastery of dialectics or physics may have eluded you, but that is no reason to despair of achieving freedom, self-respect, unselfishness, and obedience to the will of God.

68. Live out your days in untroubled serenity, refusing to be coerced though the whole world deafen you with its demands, and though wild beasts rend piecemeal this poor envelope of clay. In all that, nothing can prevent the mind from possessing itself in peace, from correctly assessing the events around it, and from making prompt use of the material thus offered; so that judgement may say to the event, 'This is what you are in essence, no matter how rumour paints you,'

1. During the reign of terror by the Thirty which succeeded the overthrow of democracy at Athens in 403 B.C., many unoffending persons were put to death. When Socrates, with four others, was commanded to arrest an honest citizen, Leon of Salamis, he sturdily refused to carry out the tyrants' bidding.

2. One of Aristophanes's many gibes at Socrates (*Clouds*, 362).

and service may say to the opportunity, 'You are what I was looking for.' The occurrence of the moment is always good material for the employment of reason and brotherliness – in a word, for the practices proper to men or gods. For not a thing ever happens but has its special pertinence to god or man; it arrives as no novel intractable problem, but as an old and serviceable friend.

69. To live each day as though one's last, never flustered, never apathetic, never attitudinizing – here is the perfection of character.

70. The gods, though they live for ever, feel no resentment at having to put up eternally with the generations of men and their misdeeds; nay more, they even show every possible care and concern for them. Are you, then, whose abiding is but for a moment, to lose patience – you who are yourself one of the culprits?

71. How ridiculous not to flee from one's own wickedness, which is possible, yet endeavour to flee from another's, which is not.

72. Whatever the reasoning and social faculty finds unthinking or unbrotherly, it can reasonably pronounce inferior to itself.

73. When you have done a good action, and another has had the benefit of it, why crave for yet more in addition – applause for your kindness, or some favour in return – as the foolish do?

74. No man tires of receiving benefits. But benefit comes from doing acts that accord with nature. Never tire, then, of receiving such benefits through the very act of conferring them.

75. Universal Nature's impulse was to create an orderly world. It follows, then, that everything now happening must follow a logical sequence; if it were not so, the prime purpose towards which the impulses of the World-Reason are directed would be an irrational one. Remembrance of this will help you to face many things more calmly.

BOOK EIGHT

1. It will tend to avert complacency if you remember that any claim to have lived as a philosopher all your life, or even since reaching manhood, is now out of the question; indeed, it is as evident to many others as it is to yourself that even today philosophy is still far beyond you. Consequently your mind remains in a state of confusion, and it grows no easier to earn the title of philosopher; also, your station in life militates constantly against it. Once all this is seen in its true light, you should banish any thoughts of how you may appear to others, and rest content if you can make the remainder of your life what nature would have it to be. Learn to understand her will, and let nothing else distract you. Up to now, all your wanderings in search of the good life have been unsuccessful; it was not to be found in the casuistries of logic, nor in wealth, celebrity, worldly pleasures, or anything else. Where, then, lies the secret? In doing what man's nature seeks. How so? By adopting strict principles for the regulation of impulse and action. Such as? Principles regarding what is good or bad for us: thus, for example, that nothing can be good for a man unless it helps to make him just, self-disciplined, courageous, and independent; and nothing bad unless it has the contrary effect.

2. Of any action, ask yourself, What will its consequences be to me? Shall I repent of it? Before long I shall be dead and all will be forgotten; but in the meantime, if this undertaking is fit for a rational and social being, who is under the same law as God himself, why look for more?

3. Alexander, Caesar, Pompey – what were they beside

Diogenes, Heraclitus, Socrates? These last looked at things and their causes and what they are made of; and their master-spirits were cast in one mould. But the others – what a host of cares, what an infinity of enslavements!

4. You may break your heart, but men will still go on as before.

5. The first rule is, to keep an untroubled spirit; for all things must bow to Nature's law, and soon enough you must vanish into nothingness, like Hadrian and Augustus. The second is to look things in the face and know them for what they are, remembering that it is your duty to be a good man. Do without flinching what man's nature demands; say what seems to you most just – though with courtesy, modesty, and sincerity.

6. Universal Nature's task is to shuffle, transpose, interchange, remove from one state and transfer to another. Everywhere there is change; and yet we need fear nothing unexpected, for all things are ruled by age-long wont, and even the manner of apportioning them does not vary.

7. Every nature finds its satisfaction in the smooth pursuance of its own road. To a nature endowed with reason, this means assenting to no impression that is misleading or obscure, giving rein to no impulse towards actions that are not social, limiting all desires or rejections to things that lie within its own power, and greeting every dispensation of Nature with an equal welcome. For these dispensations are as truly a part of her as a leaf's nature is part of the plant's; save that the leaf's is part of a nature which has no feelings or reason, and is capable of being frustrated, while man's nature is part of one which not only cannot be frustrated, but also is endowed with both intelligence and justice, since it assigns to all men

equally their proper share of time, being, causation, activity, and experiences. (Do not look to find this equality, though, in any exact correspondence between one man and another in every particular, but rather in a general comparison of them both in their entirety.)

8. You cannot hope to be a scholar. But what you can do is to curb arrogance; what you can do is to rise above pleasures and pains; you can be superior to the lure of popularity; you can keep your temper with the foolish and ungrateful, yes, and even care for them.

9. Let no one, not even yourself, ever hear you abusing court life again.

10. Repentance is remorse for the loss of some helpful opportunity. Now, what is good is always helpful, and must be the concern of every good man; but an opportunity of pleasure is something no good man would ever repent of having let pass. It follows, therefore, that pleasure is neither good nor helpful.

11. Ask yourself, What is this thing in itself, by its own special constitution? What is it in substance, and in form, and in matter? What is its function in the world? For how long does it subsist?

12. When it is hard to shake off sleep, remind yourself that to be going about the duties you owe society is to be obeying the laws of man's nature and your own constitution, whereas sleep is something we share with the unreasoning brute creation; and furthermore, that obedience to one's own nature is the more proper, the more suitable, and indeed the more agreeable course.

13. If possible, make it a habit to discover the essential

very impression, its effects on the self, and its
logical analysis.

r whom you meet, always begin by asking your-
self, What are his views on the goodness or badness of things?
For then, if his beliefs about pleasure and pain and their
causes, or about repute and disrepute, or life and death are of
a certain type, I shall not be surprised or scandalized to find
his actions in keeping with them; I shall tell myself that he
has no choice.

15. Nobody is surprised when a fig-tree brings forth figs.
Similarly, we ought to be ashamed of our surprise when the
world produces its normal crop of happenings. A physician
or a shipmaster would blush to be surprised if a patient proves
feverish, or a wind contrary.

16. To change your mind and defer to correction is not to
sacrifice your independence; for such an act is your own, in
pursuance of your own impulse, your own judgement, and
your own thinking.

17. If the choice is yours, why do the thing? If another's,
where are you to lay the blame for it? On gods? On atoms?
Either would be insanity. All thoughts of blame are out of
place. If you can, correct the offender; if not, correct the
offence; if that too is impossible, what is the point of recrimin-
ations? Nothing is worth doing pointlessly.

18. That which dies does not drop out of the world. Here it
remains; and here too, therefore, it changes and is resolved
into its several particles; that is, into the elements which go
to form the universe and yourself. They themselves likewise
undergo change, and yet from them comes no complaint.

19. Everything – a horse, a vine – is created for some duty.

This is nothing to wonder at: even the sun-god himself will tell you, 'There is a work that I am here to do,' and so will all the other sky-dwellers. For what task, then, were you yourself created? For pleasure? Can such a thought be tolerated?

20. Nature always has an end in view; and this aim includes a thing's ending as much as its beginning or its duration. She is like the ball's thrower. Is the ball itself bettered by its upward flight? Is it any worse as it comes down, or as it lies after its fall? What does a bubble gain by holding together, or lose by collapsing? The like is true of a candle, too.

21. Turn this mortal body inside out, and now see the appearance it presents. See what it comes to in old age, or sickness, or decay. How fleeting are the lives of him alike who praises and him who is praised; of the rememberer and the remembered; how small their little corner of this terrestrial zone – and even there they are not all at peace with one another. Nay, the whole earth is itself no more than the puniest dot.

22. Give it the whole of your attention, whether it be a material object, an action, a principle, or the meaning of what is being said.

This disappointment serves you right. You would rather hope for goodness tomorrow than practise it today.

23. In what I do, I am to do it with reference to the service of mankind. In what befalls me, I am to accept it with reference to the gods, and to that universal source from which the whole close-linked chain of circumstance has its issue.

24. What do the baths bring to your mind? Oil, sweat, dirt, greasy water, and everything that is disgusting. Such, then, is life in all its parts, and such is every material thing in it.

25. Death robbed Lucilla of Verus,[1] and later claimed
Lucilla too. Death took Maximus from Secunda, then
Secunda herself; Diotimus from Epitynchanus, and Epitynchanus after him; Faustina from Antoninus, and Antoninus
in his turn. So it is ever. Celer buries Hadrian, and is buried
himself. Those noble minds of old, those men of prescience,
those men of pride, where are they now? Keen wits like
Charax, Demetrius the Platonist, Eudaemon, and others like
them; all enduring but for a day, all now long since dead and
gone; some forgotten as soon as dead, some passed into
legend, some faded even out of legend itself. Bethink you
then how either this complex body of your own must also
one day be broken up in dispersion, or else the breath that
animates it must be extinguished, or removed and translated
elsewhere.

26. A man's true delight is to do the things he was made for.
He was made to show goodwill to his kind, to rise above the
promptings of his senses, to distinguish appearances from
realities, and to pursue the study of universal Nature and her
works.

27. We have three relationships: one to this bodily shell
which envelops us, one to the divine Cause which is the source
of everything in all things, and one to our fellow-mortals
around us.

1. Lucilla and Verus were Marcus's own parents. Maximus was the
teacher to whom he refers with gratitude in I, 15, and Secunda that
philosopher's wife. Epitynchanus and Diotimus are unknown. The
emperor Antoninus, who was married to Faustina, was the adoptive
father of Marcus. Celer was secretary to the emperor Hadrian. Of
Charax we know nothing. By Demetrius is perhaps meant Demetrius
of Phaleron, the last of the famous Athenian orators and statesmen,
to whom Marcus alludes again in IX, 29. Eudaemon is said to have
been an astrologer of repute.

28. Pain must be an evil either to the body – in which case let the body speak for itself – or if not, to the soul. But the soul can always refuse to consider it an evil, and so keep its skies unclouded and its calm unruffled. For there is no decision, no impulse, no movement of approach or recoil, but must proceed from within the self; and into this self no evil can force its way.

29. Erasing all fancies, keep on saying to yourself, 'It lies in my own hands to ensure that no viciousness, cupidity, or turmoil of any kind finds a home in this soul of mine; it lies with me to perceive all things in their true light, and to deal with each of them as it merits.' Remember this authority, which is nature's gift to you.

30. Both in the senate and when addressing individuals, use language that is seemly but not rhetorical. Be sane and wholesome in your speech.

31. Think of the court of Augustus: wife, daughter, children, grandsires, sister, Agrippa,[1] kindred, connexions, friends, Areius, Maecenas, medical attendants, priests – an entire court, all vanished. Turn to other records of eclipse; extinctions not of individuals but of whole stocks – the Pompeys, for example – and the inscription we see on memorials, 'The last of his house.' Think of all the pains taken by their predecessors to leave an heir after them; and yet in the end someone must be the last, and one more whole race has perished.

32. Your every separate action should contribute towards an integrated life; and if each of them, so far as it can, does

1. Agrippa and Maecenas were the two chief ministers of Augustus, having between them the management of almost all public affairs. Areius the philosopher was his personal friend and counsellor.

its part to this end, be satisfied; for that is something which nobody can prevent. 'There will be interferences from without,' you say? Even so, they will not affect the justice, prudence, and reasonableness of your intentions. 'No, but some kind of practical action may be prevented.' Perhaps; yet if you submit to the frustration with a good grace, and are sensible enough to accept what offers itself instead, you can substitute some alternative course which will be equally consistent with the integration we are speaking of.

33. Accept modestly; surrender gracefully.

34. You have perhaps seen a severed hand or foot, or a head lying by itself apart from its body. That is the state to which a man is doing his best to reduce himself, when he refuses to accept what befalls him and breaks away from his fellows, or when he acts for selfish ends alone. Then you become an outcast from the unity of Nature; though born a part of it, you have cut yourself away with your own hand. Yet here is the beautiful thought: that it still lies in your own power to reunite yourself. No other part of creation has been so favoured by God with permission to come together again, after once being sundered and divided. Behold, then, his goodness, with which he has dignified man: he has put it in his power, not only initially to keep himself inseparate from the whole, but afterwards, if separated, to return and be reunited and resume his membership as before.

35. When the Nature of all things rational equipped each rational being with his powers, one of the faculties we received from her hand was this, that just as she herself transmutes every obstacle or opposition, fits it into its place in destiny's pattern, and assimilates it into herself, so a rational

being has power to turn each hindrance into material for himself, and use it to set forward his own endeavours.

36. Never confuse yourself by visions of an entire lifetime at once. That is, do not let your thoughts range over the whole multitude and variety of the misfortunes that may befall you, but rather, as you encounter each one, ask yourself, 'What is there unendurable, so insupportable, in this?' You will find that you are ashamed to admit defeat. Again, remember that it is not the weight of the future or the past that is pressing upon you, but ever that of the present alone. Even this burden, too, can be lessened if you confine it strictly to its own limits, and are severe enough with your mind's inability to bear such a trifle.

37. Are Pantheia [1] or Pergamus still sitting to this day by the tomb of Verus? Chabrias or Diotimus by Hadrian's? Ridiculous! And supposing they were, would the dead be sensible of it? Or if sensible, pleased? Moreover, even if the dead themselves were pleased, could the mourners, for their part, be expected to go on living for ever? Were not they likewise doomed to become old men and old women, and to pass away in their turn? – and then what could the mourned do, when their mourners were no more? And all this for nothing more than a bagful of stench and corruption.

38. In the words of Crito the sage, 'If thou hast eyes to see, then see.'

39. In the constitution of a rational being, I find no virtue implanted for the combating of justice, but I do find self-control implanted for the combating of pleasure.

---

1. According to Lucian, Pantheia was the mistress, and Pergamus a freedman, of Verus, Marcus's imperial colleague.

40. Subtract your own notions of what you imagine to be painful, and then your self stands invulnerable. 'My self – what is it?' Your reason. 'But I am not all reason.' So be it; in that case, at least let your reason forbear to give pain to itself, and if another part of you is in trouble, let its thoughts about itself be its own concern.

41. To the nature of the vital force animating our bodies, any frustration of the senses is an evil, and so is the frustration of any endeavour. The nature of a plant has likewise its own frustrations and its evils; and in the same way, any frustration of the mind is an evil to the nature of the mind. Apply all this to your own case. Does a pain affect you, or a pleasure? The senses will see to that. Have you been baulked in an endeavour? It is true that if it was made without any allowance for possible failure, such frustration is indeed an evil to you as a rational being. However, once you accept that universal necessity, you can suffer no harm and no frustration. Within its own domain, there is nobody who can frustrate the mind. Fire, sword, oppression, calumny, and all else are powerless to touch it. 'The globe, once orbed and true, remains a sphere.' *

42. I, who have never wilfully pained another, have no business to pain myself.

43. To each his own felicity. For me, soundness of my sovereign faculty, reason; no shrinking from mankind and its vicissitudes; the ability to survey and accept all things with a kindly eye, and to deal with them according to their deserts.

44. Make the best of today. Those who aim instead at tomorrow's plaudits fail to remember that future generations

* Empedocles.

will be nowise different from the contemporaries who so try their patience now, and nowise less mortal. In any case, can it matter to you how the tongues of posterity may wag, or what views of yourself it may entertain?

45. Take me and cast me where you will; I shall still be possessor of the divinity within me, serene and content so long as it can feel and act as becomes its constitution. Is the matter of such moment that my soul should be afflicted by it, and changed for the worse, to become a cowering craven thing, suppliant and spiritless? Could anything at all be of such consequence as that?

46. No event can happen to a man but what is properly incidental to man's condition, nor to an ox, vine, or stone but what properly belongs to the nature of oxen, vines, and stones. Then if all things experience only what is customary and natural to them, why complain? The same Nature which is yours as well as theirs brings you nothing you cannot bear.

47. If you are distressed by anything external, the pain is not due to the thing itself but to your own estimate of it; and this you have the power to revoke at any moment. If the cause of the trouble lies in your own character, set about reforming your principles; who is there to hinder you? If it is the failure to take some apparently sound course of action that is vexing you, then why not take it, instead of fretting? 'Because there is an insuperable obstacle in the way.' In that case, do not worry; the responsibility for inaction is not yours. 'But life is not worth living with this thing undone.' Why then, bid life a good-humoured farewell; accepting the frustration gracefully, and dying like any other man whose actions have not been inhibited.

48. Remember that your higher Self becomes invincible when

once it withdraws into itself and calmly refuses to act against its will, even though such resistance may be wholly irrational. How much more, then, when its decision is based on reason and circumspection! Thus a mind that is free from passion is a very citadel; man has no stronger fortress in which to seek shelter and defy every assault. Failure to perceive this is ignorance; but to perceive it, and still not to seek its refuge, is misfortune indeed.

49. Never go beyond the sense of your original impressions. These tell you that such-and-such a person is speaking ill of you; that was their message; they did not go on to say it has done you any harm. I see my child is ill; my eyes tell me that, but they do not suggest that his life is in danger. Always, then, keep to the original impressions; supply no additions of your own, and you are safe. Or at least, add only a recognition of the great world-order by which all things are brought to pass.

50. Is your cucumber bitter? Throw it away. Are there briars in your path? Turn aside. That is enough. Do not go on to say, 'Why were things of this sort ever brought into the world?' The student of nature will only laugh at you; just as a carpenter or a shoemaker would laugh, if you found fault with the shavings and scraps from their work which you saw in the shop. Yet they, at least, have somewhere to throw their litter; whereas Nature has no such out-place. That is the miracle of her workmanship: that in spite of this self-limitation, she nevertheless transmutes into herself everything that seems worn-out or old or useless, and re-fashions it into new creations, so as never to need either fresh supplies from without, or a place to discard her refuse. Her own space, her own materials and her own skill are sufficient for her.

51. Dilatory action, incoherent conversation, vague impressions; a soul too inwardly cramped; a soul too outwardly effusive; a life without room for leisure – avoid such things. Martyrdom, mutilation, execration; how can they affect the mind's ability to remain pure, sane, temperate, just? A man may stand by a clear spring of sweet water and heap abusive words upon it, yet it still goes on welling up fresh and wholesome; he may even cast in mire and filth, but it will quickly dissolve them and wash them away, and show no stain. How be lord yourself of such a perennial fountain? By safeguarding the right to be your own master every hour of the day, in all charity, simplicity and modesty.

52. Without an understanding of the nature of the universe, a man cannot know where he is; without an understanding of its purpose, he cannot know what he is, nor what the universe itself is. Let either of these discoveries be hid from him, and he will not be able so much as to give a reason for his own existence. So what are we to think of anyone who cares to seek or shun the applause of the shouting multitudes, when they know neither where they are nor what they are?

53. Would you wish for the praise of one who thrice an hour calls down curses on his own head? Would you please one who cannot even please himself? And how can a man be pleased with himself, when he repents of well-nigh everything he does?

54. As your breathing partakes of the circumfluent air, so let your thinking partake of the circumfluent Mind. For there is a mental Force which, for him who can draw it to himself, is no less ubiquitous and all-pervading than is the atmosphere for him who can breathe it.

55. The general wickedness of mankind cannot injure the universe; nor can the particular wickedness of one man injure a fellow-man. It harms none but the culprit himself; and he can free himself from it as soon as he so chooses.

56. My neighbour's will is of no greater concern to my will than his breath or his flesh. No matter how much we are made for one another, still each man's self has its own sovereign rights. Otherwise my neighbour's wickedness would become my evil; and God has not willed this, lest the ruin of my happiness should lie at another's disposal.

57. The sun is seen to pour down and expend itself in all directions, yet is never exhausted. For this downpouring is but a self-extension; sunbeams, in fact, derive their very name from a word signifying 'to be extended'. To understand the property of a sunbeam, watch the light as it streams into a darkened room through a narrow chink. It prolongs itself forward in a straight line, until it is held up by encountering some solid body which blocks its passage to the air beyond; and then it remains at rest there, without slipping off or falling away. The emission, and the diffusion, of thought should be the counterpart of this: not exhausting, but simply extending itself; not dashing violently or furiously against the obstacles it encounters, nor yet falling away in despair; but holding its ground and lighting up that upon which it rests. Failure to transmit it is mere self-deprivation of light.

58. He who fears death either fears to lose all sensation or fears new sensations. In reality, you will either feel nothing at all, and therefore nothing evil, or else, if you can feel any new sensations, you will be a new creature, and so will not have ceased to have life.

59. Men exist for each other. Then either improve them, or put up with them.

60. An arrow travels in one fashion, but the mind in another. Even when the mind is feeling its way cautiously and working round a problem from every angle, it is still moving directly onwards and making for its goal.

61. Enter into the ruling principle of your neighbour's mind, and suffer him to enter into yours.

BOOK NINE

1. Injustice is a sin. Nature has constituted rational beings for their own mutual benefit, each to help his fellows according to their worth, and in no wise to do them hurt; and to contravene her will is plainly to sin against this eldest of all the deities. Untruthfulness, too, is a sin, and against the same goddess. For Nature is the nature of Existence itself; and existence connotes the kinship of all created beings. Truth is but another name for this Nature, the original creator of all true things. So, where a wilful lie is a sin because the deception is an act of injustice, an involuntary lie is also a sin because it is a discordant note in Nature's harmony, and creates mutinous disorder in an orderly universe. For mutinous indeed it is, when a man lets himself be carried, even involuntarily, into a position contrary to truth; seeing that he has so neglected the faculties Nature gave him that he is no longer able to distinguish the false from the true.

Again, it is a sin to pursue pleasure as a good and to avoid pain as an evil. It is bound to result in complaints that Nature is unfair in her rewarding of vice and virtue; since it is the bad who are so often in enjoyment of pleasures and the means to obtain them, while pains and events that occasion pains descend upon the heads of the good. Besides, if a man is afraid of pain, he is afraid of something happening which will be part of the appointed order of things, and this is itself a sin; if he is bent on the pursuit of pleasure, he will not stop at acts of injustice, which again is manifestly sinful. No; when Nature herself makes no distinction – and if she did, she would not have brought pains and pleasures into existence side by side – it behoves those who would follow in her footsteps to be like-minded and exhibit the same indifference. He therefore who does not view with equal unconcern pain or pleasure, death or life, fame or dishonour – all of them employed by Nature without any partiality – clearly commits a sin. And in saying that nature employs them without partiality, I mean that every successive generation of created things equally passes through the same experiences in turn; for this is the outcome of the original impulse which in the beginning moved Providence – by taking certain germs of future existences, and endowing them with productive powers of self-realization, of mutation, and of succession – to progress from the inception of the universe to its present orderly system.

2. A man of finer feelings would have taken leave of the world before ever sampling its falsehood, double-dealing, luxury, and pride; but now that all these have been tasted to satiety, the next best course would be to end your life forthwith. Or are you really resolved to go on dwelling in the midst of iniquity, and has experience not yet persuaded you to flee from the pestilence? For infection of the mind is a far more dangerous pestilence than any unwholesomeness or disorder in the atmosphere around us. Insofar as we are animals, the one attacks our lives; but as men, the other attacks our manhood.

3. Despise not death; smile, rather, at its coming; it is among the things that Nature wills. Like youth and age, like growth and maturity, like the advent of teeth, beard, and grey hairs, like begetting, pregnancy, and childbirth, like every other natural process that life's seasons bring us, so is our dissolution. Never, then, will a thinking man view death lightly, impatiently, or scornfully; he will wait for it as but one more of Nature's processes. Even as you await the baby's

emergence from the womb of your wife, so await the hour when the little soul shall glide forth from its sheath.

But if your heart would have comfort of a simpler sort, then there is no better solace in the face of death than to think on the nature of the surroundings you are leaving, and the characters you will no longer have to mix with. Not that you must find these offensive; rather, your duty is to care for them and bear with them mildly; yet never forget that you are parting from men of far other principles than your own. One thing, if any, might have held you back and bound you to life; the chance of fellowship with kindred minds. But when you contemplate the weariness of an existence in company so discordant, you cry, 'Come quickly, Death, lest I too become forgetful of myself.'

4. The sinner sins against himself; the wrongdoer wrongs himself, becoming the worse by his own action.

5. A man does not sin by commission only, but often by omission.

6. Enough if your present opinion be grounded in conviction, your present action grounded in unselfishness, and your present disposition contented with whatever befalls you from without.

7. Erase fancy; curb impulse; quench desire; let sovereign reason have the mastery.

8. A single life-principle is divided amongst all irrational creatures, and a single mind-principle distributed among the rational; just as this one earth gives form to all things earthy, and just as all of us who have sight and breath see by the self-same light and breathe of the self-same air.

9. All things that share the same element tend to seek their own kind. Things earthy gravitate towards earth, things aqueous flow towards one another, things aerial likewise – whence the need for the barriers which keep them forcibly apart. The tendency of flames is to mount skyward, because of the elemental fire; even here below, they are so eager for the company of their own kind that any sort of material, if it be reasonably dry, will ignite with ease, since there is only a minority of its ingredients which is resistant to fire. In the same way, therefore, all portions of the universal Mind are drawn towards one another. More strongly, indeed; since, being higher in the scale of creation, their eagerness to blend and combine with their affinities is proportionately keener. This instinct for reunion shows itself in its first stage among the creatures without reason, when we see bees swarming, cattle herding, birds nesting in colonies, and couples mating; because in them soul has already emerged, and in such relatively higher forms of life as theirs the desire for union is found at a level of intensity which is not present in stones or sticks. When we come to beings with reason, there are political associations, comradeships, family life, public meetings, and in times of war treaties and armistices; and among the still higher orders, a measure of unity even exists between bodies far separated from one another – as for example with the stars. Thus ascent in the ranks of creation can induce fellow-feeling even where there is no proximity.

Yet now see what happens. It is we – we, intelligent beings – who alone have forgotten this mutual zeal for unity; among us alone the currents are not seen to converge. Nevertheless, though man may flee as he will, he is still caught and held fast; Nature is too strong for him. Observe with care, and you will see: you will sooner find a fragment of earth unrelated to the rest of earth than a man who is utterly without some link with his fellows.

10. Everything bears fruit; man, God, the whole universe, each in its proper season. No matter that the phrase is restricted in common use to vines and such like. Reason, too, yields fruit, both for itself and for the world; since from it comes a harvest of other good things, themselves all bearing the stamp of reason.

11. Teach them better, if you can; if not, remember that kindliness has been given you for moments like these. The gods themselves show kindness to such men; and at times, so indulgent are they, will even aid them in their endeavours to secure health, wealth, or reputation. This you too could do; who is there to hinder you?

12. Work yourself hard, but not as if you were being made a victim, and not with any desire for sympathy or admiration. Desire one thing alone: that your actions or inactions alike should be worthy of a reasoning citizen.

13. Today I have got myself out of all my perplexities; or rather, I have got the perplexities out of myself – for they were not without, but within; they lay in my own outlook.

14. Everything is banal in experience, fleeting in duration, sordid in content; in all respects the same today as generations now dead and buried have found it to be.

15. Facts stand wholly outside our gates; they are what they are, and no more; they know nothing about themselves, and they pass no judgement upon themselves. What is it, then, that pronounces the judgement? Our own guide and ruler, Reason.

16. A rational and social being is not affected in himself for either better or worse by his feelings, but by his will; just as his outward behaviour, good or bad, is the product of will, not of feelings.

17. For the thrown stone there is no more evil in falling than there is good in rising.

18. Penetrate into their inmost minds, and you will see what manner of critics you are afraid of, and how capable they are of criticizing themselves.

19. All things are in process of change. You yourself are ceaselessly undergoing transformation, and the decay of some of your parts, and so is the whole universe.

20. Leave another's wrongdoing where it lies.

21. In the interruption of an activity, or the discontinuance and, as it were, death of an impulse, or an opinion, there is no evil. Look back at the phases of your own growth : childhood, boyhood, youth, age : each change itself a kind of death. Was this so frightening? Or take the lives you lived under your grandfather and then under your mother and then your father; trace the numerous differences and changes and discontinuances there were in those days, and ask yourself, 'Were they so frightening?' No more so, then, is the cessation, the interruption, the change from life itself.

22. Your own mind, the Mind of the universe, your neighbour's mind – be prompt to explore them all. Your own, so that you may shape it to justice; the universe's, that you may recollect what it is you are a part of; your neighbour's, that you may understand whether it is informed by ignorance or knowledge, and also may recognize that it is kin to your own.

23. As a unit yourself, you help to complete the social whole; and similarly, therefore, your every action should help to complete the social life. Any action which is not related either directly or remotely to this social end disjoints that life, and destroys its unity. It is as much the act of a schismatic as when some citizen in a community does his utmost to dissociate himself from the general accord.

24. Childish squabbles, childish games, 'petty breaths supporting corpses' – why, the ghosts in Homer have more evident reality!

25. First get at the nature and quality of the original cause, separate it from the material to which it has given shape, and study it; then determine the possible duration of its effects.

26. The woes you have had to bear are numberless because you were not content to let Reason, your guide and master, do its natural work. Come now, no more of this!

27. When those about you are venting their censure or malice upon you, or raising any other sort of injurious clamour, approach and penetrate into their souls, and see what manner of men they are. You will find little enough reason for all your painstaking efforts to win their good opinion. All the same, it still remains your duty to think kindly of them; for Nature has made them to be your friends, and even the gods themselves lend them every sort of help, by dreams and by oracles, to gain the ends on which their hearts are set.

28. Upwards and downwards,[1] from age to age, the cycles of the universe follow their unchanging round. It may be that

1. Upwards and downwards; i.e. changing successively from fire to air, air to water, water to earth, and then back again in the reverse order, as Heraclitus taught. (See page 54, note 2.)

the World-Mind wills each separate happening in succession; and if so, then accept the consequences. Or, it may be, there was but one primal act of will, of which all else is the sequel; every event being thus the germ of another. To put it another way, things are either isolated units, or they form one inseparable whole. If that whole be God, then all is well; but if aimless chance, at least you need not be aimless also.

Soon earth will cover us all. Then in time earth, too, will change; later, what issues from this change will itself in turn incessantly change, and so again will all that then takes its place, even unto the world's end. To let the mind dwell on these swiftly rolling billows of change and transformation is to know a contempt for all things mortal.

29. The primal Cause is like a river in flood; it bears everything along. How ignoble are the little men who play at politics and persuade themselves that they are acting in the true spirit of philosophy. Babes, incapable even of wiping their noses! What then, you who are a man? Why, do what nature is asking of you at this moment. Set about it as the opportunity offers, and no glancing around to see if you are observed. But do not expect Plato's ideal commonwealth; be satisfied if even a trifling endeavour comes off well, and count the result no mean success. For who can hope to alter men's convictions; and without change of conviction what can there be but grudging subjection and feigned assent? Oh yes; now go on and talk to me of Alexander, and Philip, and Demetrius of Phaleron.[1] If those men did in truth understand the will of Nature and school themselves to follow it, that is their own affair. But if it was nothing more than a stage-role they were playing, no court has condemned me to imitate their example. Philosophy is a modest profession, all simplicity

1. See page 126, note 1.

and plain dealing. Never try to seduce me into solemn pretentiousness.

30. Look down from above on the numberless herds of mankind, with their mysterious ceremonies, their divers voyagings in storm and calm, and all the chequered pattern of their comings and gatherings and goings. Go on to consider the life of bygone generations; and then the life of all those who are yet to come; and even at the present day, the life of the hordes of far-off savages. In short, reflect what multitudes there are who are ignorant of your very name; how many more will have speedily forgotten it; how many, perhaps praising you now, who will soon enough be abusing you; and that therefore remembrance, glory, and all else together are things of no worth.

31. When beset from without by circumstance, be unperturbed; when prompted from within to action, be just and fair : in fine, let both will and deed issue in behaviour that is social and fulfils the law of your being.

32. Many of the anxieties that harass you are superfluous: being but creatures of your own fancy, you can rid yourself of them and expand into an ampler region, letting your thought sweep over the entire universe, contemplating the illimitable tracts of eternity, marking the swiftness of change in each created thing, and contrasting the brief span between birth and dissolution with the endless aeons that precede the one and the infinity that follows the other.

33. A little while, and all that is before your eyes now will have perished. Those who witness its passing will go the same road themselves before long; and then what will there be to choose between the oldest grandfather and the baby that died in its cradle?

34. Observe the instincts that guide these men; the ends they struggle for; the grounds on which they like and value things. In short, picture their souls laid bare. Yet they imagine their praises or censures have weight to help or hurt. What presumption!

35. Loss is nothing else but change, and change is Nature's delight. Ever since the world began, things have been ordered by her decree in the selfsame fashion as they are at this day, and as other similar things will be ordered to the end of time. How, then, can you say that it is all amiss, and ever will be so; that no power among all the gods in heaven can avail to mend it; and that the world lies condemned to a thraldom of ills without end?

36. The substance of us all is doomed to decay; the moisture and the clay, the bones, and the fetor. Our precious marble is but a callosity of the earth, our gold and silver her sediment; our raiment shreds of hair, our purple a fish's gore; and thus with all things else. So too is the very breath of our lives – ever passing as it does from this one to that.

37. Enough of this miserable way of life, these everlasting grumbles, these monkey antics. Why must you agitate yourself so? Nothing unprecedented is happening; so what is it that disturbs you? The form of it? Take a good look at it. The matter of it? Look well at that, too. Beyond form and matter, there is nothing more. Even at this late hour, set yourself to become a simpler and better man in the sight of the gods. For the mastering of that lesson, three years are as good as a hundred.

38. If he sinned, the harm is his own. Yet perhaps, after all, he did not.

39. Either things must have their origin in one single intelligent source, and all fall into place to compose, as it were, one single body – in which case no part ought to complain of what happens for the good of the whole – or else the world is nothing but atoms and their confused minglings and dispersions. So why be so harassed? Say to the Reason at your helm, 'Come, are you dead and in decay? Is this some part you are playing? Have you sunk to the level of a beast of the field, grazing and herding with the rest?

40. The gods either have power or they have not. If they have not, why pray to them? If they have, then instead of praying to be granted or spared such-and-such a thing, why not rather pray to be delivered from dreading it, or lusting for it, or grieving over it? Clearly, if they can help a man at all, they can help him in this way. You will say, perhaps, 'But all that is something they have put in my own power.' Then surely it were better to use your power and be a free man, than to hanker like a slave and a beggar for something that is not in your power. Besides, who told you the gods never lend their aid even towards things that do lie in our own power? Begin praying in this way, and you will see. Where another man prays 'Grant that I may possess this woman,' let your own prayer be, 'Grant that I may not lust to possess her.' Where he prays, 'Grant me to be rid of such and-such a one,' you pray, 'Take from me my desire to be rid of him.' Where he begs, 'Spare me the loss of my precious child,' beg rather to be delivered from the terror of losing him. In short, give your petitions a turn in this direction, and see what comes.

41. 'When I was sick,' says Epicurus, 'I never used to talk about my bodily ailments. I did not,' he says, 'discuss any topics of that kind with my visitors. I went on dealing with

the principles of natural philosophy; and the point I particularly dwelt on was how the mind, while having its part in all these commotions of the flesh, can still remain unruffled and pursue its own proper good. Nor,' he adds, 'did I give the doctors a chance to brag of their own triumphs; my life merely went on its normal way, smoothly and happily.' In sickness, then, if you are sick, or in trouble of any other kind, be like Epicurus. Never let go your hold on philosophy for anything that may befall, and never take part in the nonsense that is talked by the ignorant and uninstructed (this is a maxim on which all schools agree). Concentrate wholly on the task before you, and on the instrument you possess for its accomplishment.

42. When you are outraged by somebody's impudence, ask yourself at once, 'Can the world exist without impudent people?' It cannot; so do not ask for impossibilities. That man is simply one of the impudent whose existence is necessary to the world. Keep the same thought present, whenever you come across roguery, double-dealing or any other form of obliquity. You have only to remind yourself that the type is indispensable, and at once you will feel kindlier towards the individual. It is also helpful if you promptly recall what special quality Nature has given us to counter such particular faults. For there are antidotes with which she has provided us: gentleness to meet brutality, for example, and other correctives for other ills. Generally speaking, too, you have the opportunity of showing the culprit his blunder – for everyone who does wrong is failing of his proper objective, and is thereby a blunderer. Besides, what harm have you suffered? Nothing has been done by any of these victims of your irritation that could hurtfully affect your own mind; and it is in the mind alone that anything evil or damaging

to the self can have reality. What is there wrong or surprising, after all, in a boor behaving boorishly? See then if it is not rather yourself you ought to blame, for not foreseeing that he would offend in this way. You, in virtue of your reason, had every means for thinking it probable that he would do so; you forgot this, and now his offence takes you by surprise. When you are indignant with anyone for his perfidy or ingratitude, turn your thoughts first and foremost upon yourself. For the error is clearly your own, if you have put any faith in the good faith of a man of that stamp, or, when you have done him a kindness, if it was not done unreservedly and in the belief that the action would be its own full reward. Once you have done a man a service, what more would you have? Is it not enough to have obeyed the laws of your own nature, without expecting to be paid for it? That is like the eye demanding a reward for seeing, or the feet for walking. It is for that very purpose that they exist; and they have their due in doing what they were created to do. Similarly, man is born for deeds of kindness; and when he has done a kindly action, or otherwise served the common welfare, he has done what he was made for, and has received his quittance.

BOOK TEN

1. O soul of mine, will you never be good and sincere, all one, all open, visible to the beholder more clearly than even your encompassing body of flesh? Will you never taste the sweetness of a loving and affectionate heart? Will you never be filled full and unwanting; craving nothing, yearning for no creature or thing to minister to your pleasures, no prolongation of days to enjoy them, no place or country or pleasant clime or sweet human company? When will you be content with your present state, happy in all about you, persuaded that all things are yours, that all comes from the gods, and that all is and shall be well with you, so long as it is their good pleasure and ordained by them for the safety and welfare of that perfect living Whole – so good, so just, so beautiful – which gives life to all things, upholding and enfolding them, and at their dissolution gathering them into Itself so that yet others of their kind may spring forth? Will you never be fit for such fellowship with gods and men as to have no syllable of complaint against them, and no syllable of reproach from them?

2. Pay heed to what your particular nature requires of you, like one who is wholly under great Nature's governance. Do it and accept it, provided always that it promise no harm to your physical nature. Yet pay heed also to the requirements of that physical nature, and give assent to them all, unless they in turn promise harm to the rational nature (and by the rational is directly implied the social as well). Observe these rules, without wasting pains on other things.

3. Whatever befalls, Nature has either prepared you to face

it or she has not. If something untoward happens which is within your powers of endurance, do not resent it, but bear it as she has enabled you to do. Should it exceed those powers, still do not give way to resentment; for its victory over you will put an end to its own existence. Remember, however, that in fact Nature has given you the ability to bear anything which your own judgement succeeds in declaring bearable and endurable by regarding it as a point of self-interest and duty to do so.

4. If a man makes a slip, admonish him gently and show him his mistake. If you fail to convince him, blame yourself, or else blame nobody.

5. Whatever may happen to you was prepared for you in advance from the beginning of time. In the woven tapestry of causation, the thread of your being had been intertwined from all time with that particular incident.

6. No matter whether the universe is a confusion of atoms or a natural growth, let my first conviction be that I am part of a Whole which is under Nature's governance; and my second, that a bond of kinship exists between myself and all other similar parts. If I bear these two thoughts in mind, then in the first place, being a part, I shall not feel aggrieved by any dispensation assigned to me from the Whole; since nothing which is beneficial for any whole can ever be harmful to a part, and in this case there is nothing contained in this Whole which is not beneficial to itself. (The same, indeed, could be said of every natural organism; but the nature of the universe has the further distinction that there is no cause outside itself which could ever compel it to produce anything harmful to itself.) In the remembrance, then, that I am a part of such a Whole, I shall cheerfully accept whatever may be

my lot. In the second place, inasmuch as there is this bond of kinship between myself and my fellow-parts, I shall do nothing that might injure their common welfare, but keep those kindred parts always purposefully in view, directing every impulse towards their good and away from anything that runs counter to it. Thus doing, I cannot but find the current of my life flowing smoothly; as smoothly as we may imagine that of some public man whose actions are consistently serviceable to his fellow-townsfolk, and who is ready to welcome whatever task his city may assign him.

7. All parts of the Whole – by which I mean everything naturally comprehended in the universe – must in time decay; or to speak accurately, must suffer a change of form. If by its nature this change, besides being inevitable, were to be a positive evil to them, the smooth working of the Whole could never go on; for its parts are always heading towards some change of form or other, and are all constitutionally liable to decay in their respective ways. Did Nature, then, deliberately mean to inflict injury on things which are parts of herself, making them not simply liable to evil but inescapably doomed to it; or can it be that such things happen without her knowledge? Neither supposition merits any credence. Even supposing we leave Nature herself out of account altogether, and explain all this in terms of the normal order of creation, it is still absurd to say that this mutability of the parts of the Whole is normal if at the same time we are to feel as astonished or resentful at it as though it were some unnatural occurrence; the more so, since all that the parts are doing is merely to dissolve back into the constituents of their original composition. For after all, if dissolution is not simply a mere dispersion of the elements of which I am compounded, it must be a change of the grosser particles into earth-form,

and the spiritual into air-form, so that they can all be re-absorbed into the universal Reason (no matter whether this is to be periodically consumed in flames, or to keep on perpetually renewing itself through eternal cycles of change). Observe, however, that these particles, gross and spiritual, must not be imagined to be those which we received at birth; seeing that our entire present structure has derived its increment from meats eaten and air breathed no longer ago than yesterday or the day before. What will undergo these changes, therefore, is not something our mother bore originally, but something we have received since. (Even if we admit that birth does, in fact, implicate us in great measure with these intrinsically mutable particles, I do not think it affects what I have said.)

8. If you claim for yourself such epithets as good, modest, truthful, clear-minded, right-minded, high-minded, be careful not to belie them; and if you should happen to forfeit them, lose no time in recovering them again. But remember that 'clear-mindedness' ought to suggest to you a discriminating consideration of each separate detail and a watchful attention to it; 'right-mindedness' a willing acceptance of all that Nature allots you; and 'high-mindedness' an elevation of the intellect above the workings of the flesh, be they smooth or harsh, and above vainglory, death or any other such distractions. Live up to these designations – though without craving to have them applied to you by others – and you will be a different man and enter upon a different life. To go on in your present state, continuing to be torn and soiled by an existence like this, is the way of a fool and a faint-heart; it smacks of the swordsman who has been mangled by beasts in the arena and covered with blood and bruises, and yet still pleads to be kept till the morrow, when he will only be flung

again, wounds and all, to the same teeth and claws. So step on board this little raft of attributes, and if you can contrive it, stay there as though transported to the Isles of the Blest. But if you feel yourself drifting and unable to hold your course, pluck up heart and make for some quiet haven where you will be able to hold your own; or even bid farewell to life altogether, not in a passion but simply, freely, and unassumingly, with at least this one success in life to your credit, a seemly departure from it. In order to keep those attributes ever in mind, it will help greatly not to forget the gods; to remember that what they desire is not to be flattered but that everything which has reason should become like themselves; and also to recollect that a fig-tree is that which does a fig-tree's work, a dog that which does a dog's, a bee a bee's – and a man a man's.

9. Day by day the buffoonery, quarrelling, timidity, slothfulness, and servility that surround you will conspire to efface from your mind those hallowed maxims it apprehends so unphilosophically and dismisses so carelessly. What duty requires of you is to observe each single thing and perform each action in such a manner that, while the practical demands of a situation are fully met, the powers of thought are at the same time fully exercised; and also to maintain (in reserve, but never lost to sight) the self-confidence of one who has mastered every relevant detail. Are you never going to attain to the happiness of a real integrity and dignity? Of an understanding which comprehends the inmost being of each thing, its place in the world-order, the term of its natural existence, the structure of its composition, and to whom it belongs or who has the power of bestowing or withdrawing it?

10. A spider is proud of catching a fly; so is one man of

trapping a hare, or another of netting a sprat, or a third of capturing boars or bears or Sarmatians.[1] If you go into the question of principles, are these anything but robbers one and all?

11. Make a habit of regularly observing the universal process of change; be assiduous in your attention to it, and school yourself thoroughly in this branch of study; there is nothing more elevating to the mind. For when a man realizes that at any moment he may have to leave everything behind him and depart from the company of his fellows, he casts off the body and thenceforward dedicates himself wholly to the service of justice in his personal actions and compliance with Nature in all else. No thought is wasted on what others may say or think of him or practise against him; two things alone suffice him, justice in his daily doings and contentment with all fate's apportionings. Every care, every distraction is laid aside; his only ambition is to walk in the straight paths of law, and by so doing to become a follower of God.

12. What need for guesswork when the way of duty lies there before your eyes? If the road be clear to see, go forward with a good will and no turning back; if not, wait and take the best advice you can. Should further obstacles arise, advance discreetly to the limit of your resources, always following where justice seems to point the way. To achieve justice is the summit of success, since it is herein that failure most often occurs.

13. Begin the day by asking yourself, Can the just and right conduct of another make any difference in myself? It cannot. Men who are arrogantly ready with their praise or censure, remember, are the same in their private lives, in bed and at board; recall the things they do, the things they avoid or run

1. A generic name for the tribesmen of the Danubian regions, with whom Marcus and his legions waged an almost continual warfare.

after, and the thieveries and depredations they commit – not indeed with hands and feet, but with that most precious of all their possessions, which, if a man but will it so, is the source of faith, modesty, truth, law, and the good estate of the divinity within him.

14. To Nature, whence all things come and whither all return, the cry of the humble and well-instructed heart is, 'Give as thou wilt, take back as thou wilt;' yet uttered with no heroics, but in pure obedience and goodwill.

15. Now your remaining years are few. Live them, then, as though on a mountain-top. Whether a man's lot be cast in this place or in that matters nothing, provided that in all places he views the world as a city and himself its citizen. Give men the chance to see and know a true man, living by Nature's law. If they cannot brook the sight, let them do away with him. Better so, than to live as they live.

16. Waste no more time arguing what a good man should be. Be one.

17. Let your mind constantly dwell on all Time and all Being, and thus learn that each separate thing is but as a grain of sand in comparison with Being, and as a single screw's-turn in comparison with Time.

18. Realize the nature of all things material, observing how each of them is even now undergoing dissolution and change, and is already in process of decay, or dispersion, or whatever other natural fate may be in store for it.

19. Eating, sleeping, copulating, excreting, and the like; what a crew they are! How pompous in their arrogance, how over-bearing and tyrannical, how superciliously censorious of others! A moment ago, how many feet they were licking –

and for such ends! – a moment more, and they will be doing the same again.

20. For every man and every thing, that which Nature brings makes for their own good; moreover, makes for their good at the precise moment when it is brought.

21. 'Earth is in love with the showers from above,
And the all-holy Heaven itself is in love' *

– that is, the universe is truly in love with its task of fashioning whatever is next to be; and to the universe, therefore, my response must be, 'As thou lovest, so I too love.' (Is not the same notion implied in the common saying that such-and-such a thing 'loves to happen'?)

22. Either you go on living here, to which custom has sufficiently seasoned you by now; or you remove elsewhere, which you do of your own free election; or you die, which means that your service is at an end. Other choice there can be none; so put a good face on it.

23. Let it be clear to you that the peace of green fields can always be yours, in this, that, or any other spot; and that nothing is any different here from what it would be either up in the hills, or down by the sea, or wherever else you will. You will find the same thought in Plato, where he speaks of living within the city walls 'as though milking his flocks in a mountain sheepfold'.†

24. What is my master-reason to me? What am I making of it at this moment? To what use am I putting it? Is it showing itself devoid of sense? Is it becoming divorced and dissevered from the ties of fellowship? Has it grown so

* Euripides, Frag. 890.
† *Theaetetus*, 174 D

involved and so identified with the flesh as to reflect that flesh's veerings and vacillations?

25. A servant who breaks loose from his master is a runaway. For us, our master is law; and consequently any law-breaker must be a runaway. But grief, anger, or fear are all of them rejections of something which, in the past or the present or the future, has been decreed by the power that directs the universe – in other words, by Law, which allots to every creature its due.[1] To give way to fear or grief or anger, therefore, is to be a runaway.

26. A man drops seed into the womb and passes on; there-after another cause takes it up, sets to work, and brings to perfection a baby – what a transformation! The same man puts food down his throat, and once more some other cause takes it over and converts it into sensation and motion and, in short, into life, vigour, and other products both many and various. Consider these processes, which are wrought out in such mysterious ways; and discern the power at work there, in the same way as we discern the forces which attract objects earthwards or upwards – not with the eye, that is, and yet no less clearly.

27. Reflect often how all the life of today is a repetition of the past; and observe that it also presages what is to come. Review the many complete dramas and their settings, all so similar, which you have known in your own experience, or from bygone history: the whole court-circle of Hadrian, for example, or the court of Antoninus, or the courts of Philip, Alexander, and Croesus. The performance is always the same; it is only the actors who change.

1. The Greek word for law (*nomos*) was supposed to be derived from a verb meaning to allot (*nemein*).

28. When you see a man showing annoyance or resentment at anything, think of a pig kicking and squealing under the sacrificial knife. Another who takes to his couch in solitude, silently lamenting over our thraldom, is in no better case. Reasonable beings alone are granted the power of a willing conformity with circumstance; the bare conformity by itself stern necessity exacts from every created thing.

29. Whatever you take in hand, pause at every step to ask yourself, 'Is it the thought of forfeiting this that makes me dread death?'

30. When another's fault offends you, turn to yourself and consider what similar shortcomings are found in you. Do you, too, find your good in riches, pleasure, reputation, or such like? Think of this, and your anger will soon be forgotten in the reflection that he is only acting under pressure; what else could he do? Alternatively, if you are able, contrive his release from that pressure.

31. Let the sight of Satyron call up a vision of the dead Socraticus, or Eutyches, or Hymen; the sight of Euphrates bring to mind Eutychion or Silvanus; a look at Alciphron suggest the memory of Tropaeophorus; a glance at Severus, that of Crito or Xenophon; when you see yourself, think of the emperors who preceded you. Thus, with every man, imagine his counterpart; and then go on to the reflection, 'Where are they all now?' Nowhere – or anywhere. In this way, you will grow accustomed to looking on all that is mortal as vapour and nothingness; and the more so, if you will also remember that things once changed are for ever past recall. Then why struggle and strain, instead of being content to live out your little span in seemly fashion? Think what materials and possibilities for good you are rejecting; since what are all your

tribulations but exercises for the training of your reason, once it has learnt to see the truths of life in a proper philosophic light? Be patient, then, until you have made them familiar and natural to yourself, in the same way as a strong stomach can assimilate every kind of diet, or a bright fire turn anything that is cast upon it into heat and flame.

32. Let no one have the right to say truthfully of you that you are without integrity or goodness; should any think such thoughts, see that they are without foundation. This all depends upon yourself, for who else can hinder you from attaining goodness and integrity? If you cannot live so, you need only resolve to live no longer; for in that case not even reason itself could require your continuance.

33. What is the very best that can be said or done with the materials at your disposal? Be it what it may, you have the power to say it or do it; let there be no pretence that you are not a free agent. These repinings of yours will be endless until such time as the doing of a man's natural duty with whatever materials come to hand means as much to you as his pleasures mean to the voluptuary. (Indeed, every exercise of our proper natural instincts ought to be esteemed a form of pleasure; and the opportunities for this are everywhere present.) A roller, to be sure, has not always the privilege of moving at will, nor has water, nor fire, nor anything else that is under the governance of its own nature or of a soul without reason; for there are many factors which intervene to prevent it. But a mind and a reason can make their way through any obstacles, as their nature enables them and their will prompts them to do. Figure to yourself how reason finds a way past every barrier as effortlessly as fire mounts upward, or a stone falls, or a roller descends a slope; and be content to ask no more. Interferences, in any case, must either affect

the body alone – which is but an inanimate thing – or else be impotent to crush or injure us unless assisted by our own preconceptions and the surrender of reason itself. If it were otherwise, their effect on the subject would be harmful; and though we know that throughout the rest of creation the occurrence of any mishap involves some worsening of its victim, yet in the case of a man we may even say that he becomes better and more praiseworthy by the right uses which he makes of adversity. In short, never forget that nothing can injure the true citizen if it does not injure the city itself, and nothing can injure the city unless it injures law. What we call mischances do no injury to law, and therefore cannot harm either city or citizen.

34. When true principles have once been etched into the mind, even the briefest commonplace will suffice to recall the futility of regrets or fears; such as, for example,

'What are the children of men, but as leaves that drop at the wind's breath?' *

Just such leaves were those beloved children of yours; leaves, too, are the multitudes, those would-be-convincing voices that scream their plaudits, hurl their curses, or sneer and scoff in secret; leaves, again, are all they into whose hands your fame shall fall hereafter. One and all, they 'flower in the season of springtime', the gales lay them low, and anon the forest puts forth new verdure in their room. Impermanence is the badge of each and every one; and yet you chase after them, or flee from them, as though they were to endure for all eternity. A short time, and your eyes will close; and for the man who bears you to your grave, too, the tears will soon enough be falling.

* Homer, *Iliad*, vi, 147.

35. The business of a healthy eye is to see everything that is visible, not to demand no colour but green, for that merely marks a disordered vision. Likewise hearing and scent, if healthy, should be alert for all kinds of sounds and odours, and a healthy stomach for all manner of meats, like a mill which accepts whatever grist it was fashioned to grind. In the same way, then, a healthy mind ought to be prepared for anything that may befall. A mind crying 'O that my children may be spared,' or 'O that the world might ring with praises of my every act,' is an eye craving for greenery, or a tooth craving for softness.

36. No man is so fortunate but that some who stand beside his death-bed will be hailing the coming loss with delight. He was virtuous, let us say, and wise; even so, will there not be one at the end who murmurs under his breath, 'At last we can breathe freely again, without our master! To be sure, he was never harsh with any of us; but I always felt that he had a silent contempt for us'? Such is the fate of the virtuous; as for the rest of us, what a host of other good reasons there are to make not a few of our friends glad to be rid of us! Think of this when you come to die; it will ease your passing to reflect, 'I am leaving a world in which the very companions I have so toiled for, prayed for and thought for, themselves wish me gone, and hope to win some relief thereby; then how can any man cling to a lengthening of his days therein?' Yet do not on that account leave with any diminished kindness for them; maintain your own accustomed friendliness, good-will, and charity; and do not feel the departure to be a wrench, but let your leave-taking be like those painless deaths in which the soul glides easily forth from the body. Before, Nature had joined you to these men and made you one with them; now she looses the tie. I am loosed, then, as from my

own kinsfolk; yet all unresisting, and all unforced; it is simply one more of Nature's ways.

37. At every action, no matter by whom performed, make it a practice to ask yourself, 'What is his object in doing this?' But begin with yourself; put this question to yourself first of all.

38. Remember, it is the secret force hidden deep within us that manipulates our strings; there lies the voice of persuasion, there the very life, there, we might even say, is the man himself. Never confuse it in your imagination with its surrounding case of flesh, or the organs adhering thereto, which save that they grow upon the body, are as much mere instruments as the carpenter's axe. Without the agency that prompts or restrains their motions, the parts themselves are of no more service than her shuttle to the weaver, his pen to the writer, or his whip to the wagoner.

BOOK ELEVEN

1. The properties of a rational soul are these. She can contemplate herself, analyse herself, make of herself what she will, herself enjoy the fruit she bears (whereas the fruit produced by trees, like its counterpart produced by animals, is enjoyed by others), and always have her work perfectly complete at whatever moment our life reaches its appointed limit. For, unlike dances or plays or such like, where if they are suddenly cut short the performance as a whole is left imperfect, the soul, no matter at what stage arrested, will have her task complete to her own satisfaction, and be able to say, 'I am in the fullest possession of mine own.' Moreover, she can encompass the whole universe at will, both its own structure and the void surrounding it, and can reach out into eternity, embracing and comprehending the great cyclic renewals of creation, and thereby perceiving that future generations will have nothing new to witness, even as our forefathers beheld nothing more than we of today, but that if a man comes to his fortieth year, and has any understanding at all, he has virtually seen – thanks to their similarity – all possible happenings, both past and to come. Finally, the qualities of the rational soul include love of neighbours, truthfulness, modesty, and a reverence for herself before all else; and since this last is one of the qualities of law also, it follows that the principle of rationality is one and the same as the principle of justice.

2. You can soon become indifferent to the seductions of song or dance or athletic displays if you resolve the melody into its several notes, and ask yourself of each one in turn, 'Is it

this that I cannot resist?' You will flinch from admitting it. Do the same to each movement or attitude of the dancers, and similarly with the athletes. In short, save in the case of virtue and its implications, always remember to go straight for the parts themselves, and by dissecting these achieve your disenchantment. And now, transfer this method to life as a whole.

3. Happy the soul which, at whatever moment the call comes for release from the body, is equally ready to face extinction, dispersion, or survival. Such preparedness, however, must be the outcome of its own decision; a decision not prompted by mere contumacy, as with the Christians,[1] but formed with deliberation and gravity and, if it is to be convincing to others, with an absence of all heroics.

4. Have I done an unselfish thing? Well then, I have my reward. Keep this thought ever present, and persevere.

5. What is your trade? Goodness. But how are you to make a success of it unless you have a philosopher's insight into the nature of the universe, and into the particular constitution of man?

6. Drama in its earliest phase took the form of Tragedy, which by its presentation of the vicissitudes of life reminds us how naturally things of that kind can happen, and that, since they move us to pleasure on the stage, we have no

---

1. If these words are authentic and not a later insertion, they are the only reference which Marcus makes to the Christians. C. R. Haines, however, in the Loeb edition of the *Meditations*, points out that the clause is 'outside the construction, and in fact ungrammatical. It is in the very form of a marginal note, and has every appearance of being a gloss foisted into the text.'

right to be aggrieved by their occurrence on the larger stage of reality. For in these plays we are shown that, though actions must have their inevitable consequences, men can still endure them, despite the anguished 'Ah, Cithaeron!'[1] that breaks from their lips. Moreover, there are helpful sayings to be found here and there in the tragic writers; notably,

> If Heav'n care nought for me and my two boys,[2]
> There must be some good reason even for this,

or again,

> Vex not thy spirit at the course of things,

or,

> Like ears of corn the lives of men are reaped,

and many another of the kind.

After tragedy came the Old Comedy,[3] with a tongue unsparing as a schoolmaster's, but administering a wholesale rebuke to pride by its very outspokenness (which to some extent was adopted by Diogenes for the same purpose). But

---

1. In Sophocles' tragedy *Oedipus Rex* the king, in the agonized realization of his guilt and with the blood streaming from his self-mutilated eyeballs, cries, 'Ah, Cithaeron, Cithaeron, why didst thou harbour me? Why didst thou not take me and slay me out of hand?' It was on the mountain ranges of Cithaeron, near Thebes, that he had been exposed at birth by his mother Jocasta.

2. This, and the other lines quoted here, seem to have had a special place in the memory of Marcus, who had lost four of his own children. He has cited them before, in VII, 41, where the references may be found in the footnotes.

3. The three great Attic poets of what is called the 'Old Comedy', in the age of Pericles, were Cratinus and his younger contemporaries Eupolis and Aristophanes. The works of all but Aristophanes are lost; and in the words of the historian Grote, if we had not these before us, 'it would have been impossible to imagine the unmeasured and unsparing licence of attack assumed by the Old Comedy upon the gods, the institutions, the politicians, philosophers, poets, private citizens and even the women of Athens.'

later, look at the aims of the Middle Comedy [1]; and eventually of the New Comedy,[2] which was so soon to decline into the mere artificiality of the Mime.[3] To be sure, even these later writers have a few good things to say, as we all know; but what does the whole scope and intention of all their output of poetry and drama amount to?

7. Manifestly, no condition of life could be so well adapted for the practice of philosophy as this in which chance finds you today!

8. A branch severed from an adjoining branch necessarily becomes severed from the whole tree. A man, likewise, who has been divided from any of his fellows has thereby fallen

1. Towards the end of Aristophanes' career the licence of the Old Comedy was restricted by law, and writers also began to dispense with the costly services of a chorus; thus making way for the Middle Comedy (c. 400–388 B.C.), from which the chorus has disappeared and in which stock types – the soldier, the miser, the courtesan – take the place of living individuals as the subjects of ridicule. The leading authors of this period, after Aristophanes himself, are said to have been Eubulus, Antiphanes, and Alexis.

2. The New Comedy arose after Athens had become subject to the power of Macedonia, and was a further development of the Middle. Politics were excluded from the stage, and the amorous intrigues of fictitious characters became the chief theme. In this class of writers the outstanding figure is Menander, who wrote upwards of a hundred comedies and was confessedly imitated by the Roman poets Plautus and Terence.

3. Both in Greece and Rome regular comedy was always less enjoyed by the populace than the Mimes, in which the action was portrayed by the movements and gestures of a single performer while a chorus recited the accompanying text. The mimes of Sophron (c. 420 B.C.) long remained a favourite amusement of the Greeks; and at Rome this type of entertainment became so popular under Augustus and his successors that in the end it virtually superseded the legitimate theatre.

away from the whole community. But whereas the branch is lopped by some other hand, the man, by his feelings of hatred or aversion, brings about his own estrangement from his neighbour, and does not see that at the same time he has cut himself off from the whole framework of society. Nevertheless it is in our power, by grace of Zeus the author of all fellowship, to grow back and become one with our neighbour again, so playing our part once more in the integration of the whole. Yet if such acts of secession are repeated frequently, they make it difficult for the recusant to achieve this reunion and restitution. A branch which has been partner of the tree's growth since the beginning, and has never ceased to share its life, is a different thing from one that has been grafted in again after a severance. As the gardeners say, it is of the same tree, but not of the same mind.

9. Though men may hinder you from following the paths of reason, they can never succeed in deflecting you from sound action; but make sure that they are equally unsuccessful in destroying your charitable feelings towards them. You must defend both positions alike : your firmness in decision and action, and at the same time your gentleness to those who try to obstruct or otherwise molest you. It would be as great a weakness to give way to your exasperation with them as it would be to abandon your course of action and be browbeaten into surrender. In either event the post of duty is deserted; in the one case through lack of courage, and in the other through alienation from men who are your natural brothers and friends.

10. Any form of nature always outrivals art, since every art is no more than an imitation of the natural. This being so, that supreme Nature which is more perfect and all-inclusive than any other cannot fail to be pre-eminent in the artist's craft.

Furthermore, it is only with an eye on something higher that the arts produce their inferior works; and this is what Nature herself also does. Here, then, we find the origins of justice; for all the other virtues depend on this. We can never achieve true justice while we set our hearts on things of lesser value, and are content to remain credulous, headstrong, and inconstant.

11. It may be that the things you fret and fume to pursue or avoid do not come to you, but rather you go to them. Let your judgements of them, then, remain in suppression; they for their part will make no move, and so you will not be seen pursuing or avoiding them.

12. The soul attains her perfectly rounded form [1] when she is neither straining out after something nor shrinking back into herself; neither disseminating herself piecemeal nor yet sinking down in collapse; but is bathed in a radiance which reveals to her the world and herself in their true colours.

13. Will any one sneer at me? That will be his concern; mine will be to ensure that nothing I do or say shall deserve the sneer. Will he perhaps hate me? Again, his concern. Mine, to be in friendship and charity with all men, ready to show this very man himself where he is mistaken, and to do so without recrimination or ostentatious forbearance, but – if we may assume that his words were not mere cant – as frankly and generously as Phocion of old. [2] That is the right spirit for

1. This figure of a sphere, symbolizing completeness and perfection, is a favourite with Marcus; compare VIII, 41, and XII, 3 (where he attributes the metaphor to Empedocles). Horace similarly describes the good man as '*totus teres atque rotundus*' (Satires II, 7, 86).

2. An Athenian general and statesman, accused of treachery and condemned to death by the people. Asked if he had any last words to say, he replied: 'Only that I have no grudge against the Athenians.'

a man to have within him; he should never be seen by the gods in the act of harbouring a grudge or making a grievance of his sufferings. What ill can touch you if you follow the proper laws of your being and accept moment by moment whatever great Nature deems opportune, like a true man who is bent on furthering by any and every means the welfare of the world?

14. They despise and yet fawn on one another; each would outstrip the other, and yet cowers and cringes before him.

15. How hollow and insincere it sounds when someone says, 'I am determined to be perfectly straightforward with you.' Why, man, what is all this? The thing needs no prologue; it will declare itself. It should be written on your forehead, it should echo in the tones of your voice, it should shine out in a moment from your eyes, just as a single glance from the beloved tells all to the lover. Sincerity and goodness ought to have their own unmistakable odour, so that one who encounters this becomes straightway aware of it despite himself. A candour affected is a dagger concealed. The feigned friendship of the wolf is the most contemptible of all, and to be shunned beyond everything. A man who is truly good and sincere and well-meaning will show it by his looks, and no one can fail to see it.

16. The good life can be achieved to perfection by any soul capable of showing indifference to the things that are themselves indifferent. This can be done by giving careful scrutiny first to the elements that compose them, and then to the things themselves; bearing also in mind that none of them is responsible for the opinion we form of it. They make no approaches to us, they remain stationary; it is we who produce judgements about them, and proceed to inscribe these, so to speak,

in our minds; despite the fact that it is perfectly in our power either to inscribe nothing at all, or at least to delete promptly anything that may have inscribed itself unawares. Moreover, you must remember that there will not be much more time in which to give heed to these matters, and that our race will soon be run. Do not be aggrieved, then, if things are not always to your liking. As long as they are in accord with nature, be glad of them, and do not make difficulties; if they are not, then find out what your own nature itself enjoins, and make the best of your way towards that; for a man is always justified in seeking his own good.

17. Consider where each thing originates, what goes into its composition, what it is changing into, what it is going to be after the change, and that it will be no whit the worse for it.

18. *When offended*. Counsel the First. Remember the close bond between myself and the rest of mankind. This obtains, because all of us were born for one another; or to give a different reason, because I was born to be their leader, as the ram is made to lead the flock or the bull the herd; or again – to go back to the first principles – because the world, if it is not mere atoms, must be governed by Nature, and in that case the lower orders of creation must exist for the higher and the higher must exist for one another.

A Second. Think of their characters, at board and in bed and so forth; and in particular, of the pressure which their own ways of thinking exert upon them, and the consequent self-assurance with which they commit these acts of theirs.

A Third. If what they are doing is right, you have no claim to be annoyed; if it is not, it can only be unintentional and unwitting. For just as 'no soul ever wilfully foregoes truth,' so none ever wilfully denies another the treatment he is entitled to; witness their indignation if anyone accuses them of injustice, ingratitude, meanness, or any other sort of misdemeanour towards their neighbours.

A Fourth. You yourself offend in various ways, and are no different from them. You may indeed avoid certain faults, yet the inclination is there nevertheless, even if cowardice or a regard for your reputation or some such ignoble motive has restrained you from imitating their misdeeds.

A Fifth. You have no assurance that they are doing wrong at all, for the motives of men's actions are not always what they seem. There is generally much to learn before any judgement can be pronounced with certainty on another's doings.

A Sixth. Tell yourself, when you feel exasperated and out of all patience, that this mortal life endures but a moment; it will not be long before we shall one and all have been laid to rest.

A Seventh. It is not the deeds of these men – which are the concern of their own directing reason – that are the source of our annoyance, but the colour we ourselves put upon them. Eliminate this, consent to withdraw all thoughts of their heinousness, and anger disappears at once. How effect such erasure? By the reflection that you, at least, have been left undisgraced. For, were it not that nothing is bad but moral disgrace, you would be guilty of a host of malpractices yourself – robbery, and every other sort of villainy.[1]

An Eighth. Our anger and annoyance are more detrimental to us than the things themselves which anger or annoy us.

A Ninth. Kindness is irresistible, so long as it be genuine

1. Marcus has already pointed out (x, 10) that the suppression of the weaker by the stronger is always, strictly speaking, an act of robbery; though it may often take forms which are in no sense morally disgraceful. If such suppression were *eo ipso* disgraceful, it would be an evil; and Marcus himself would be guilty of much evil, in the mere performance of his imperial duties as judge and warrior.

and without false smiles or duplicity. The most consummate impudence can do nothing, if you remain persistently kind to the offender, give him a gentle word of admonition when opportunity offers, and at the moment when he is about to vent his malice upon you bring him round quietly with 'No, my son; it was not for this that we were made. I shall not be hurt; it is yourself you are hurting.' Point out courteously and in general terms how this is so, and how even bees and other gregarious animals do not behave as he does – but do it without any sarcasm or fault-finding, in real affection and with a heart free from rancour; not in the manner of a school-master, nor yet for the admiration of the bystanders, but, even though others may be present, as if you and he were alone in private.

Keep these nine counsels in your memory, as so many gifts from the Muses; and while life is still with you, begin at last to be a man. Yet in guarding yourself against anger with others, be no less careful to avoid any toadying; one is as much against the common welfare as the other, and both lead to mischief. In moments of anger, let the thought always be present that loss of temper is no sign of manliness, but that there is more virility, as well as more natural humanity, in one who shows himself gentle and peaceable; he it is who gives proof of strength and nerve and manliness, not his angry and discontented fellow. Anger is as much a mark of weakness as is grief; in both of them men receive a wound, and submit to a defeat.

In addition, take this, if you will, as a tenth gift; this time from the very leader [1] of the Muses himself. To expect bad men never to do bad things is insensate; it is hoping for the impossible. To tolerate their offences against others, and

1. Apollo, god of the lyre, presided over the nine Muses who were the inspiring divinities of poetry, music, and the arts.

expect none against yourself, is both irrational and arbitrary.

19. There are four aberrations of your soul's helmsman which you must constantly guard against, and suppress whenever detected. Say to them one by one, 'This is a thought which is not necessary,' 'This is one which would undermine fellowship,' 'This is not the voice of my true self' (for to speak anything but your true sentiments, remember, is of all things the most misplaced), and, fourthly, when you are tempted into self-reproach, 'This would prove the divine element in me to have been discomfited and forced to its knees by the ignoble and perishable flesh with its gross conceptions.'

20. Although the natural propensity of any aerial and igneous particles in your composition is to soar upwards, nevertheless in obedience to the ordinances of the Whole these are held down under restraint within the body they compose. On the other hand, all the earthy and fluid particles in you, despite their tendency to sink downwards, are held up, and made to occupy a position which is not natural to them. Thus even these particles obey the laws of the Whole; when assigned to a position, they perforce remain there until the signal for dissolution recalls them once again. Is it not grievous, then, that the only part of you which is not obedient, and chafes at its appointed sphere, should be the thinking part? Nothing violent is demanded of it, nothing but what accords with its own nature; yet it will not submit, but breaks away in the contrary direction – for what are all its movements towards injustice, intemperance, anger, grief, or fear, but wilful divergences from nature? When once the helmsman of the soul exhibits resentment at anything which happens to it, that instant it quits its post; for it was no less made for holiness and for reverence for the gods than for justice, and these,

being part of the idea of the fellowship of the universe, must come even before justice.

21. If a man's life has no consistent and uniform aim, it cannot itself remain consistent or uniform. Yet that statement does not go far enough unless you can also add something of what the aim should be. Now, it is not upon the whole range of the things which are generally assumed to be good that we find uniformity of opinion to exist, but only upon things of a certain kind: namely, those which affect the welfare of society. Accordingly, the aim we should propose to ourselves must be the benefit of our fellows and the community. Whoso directs his every effort to this will be imparting a uniformity to all his actions, and so will achieve consistency with himself.

22. Remember the country mouse's encounter with the town mouse,[1] and the flurry and agitation into which it threw him.

23. Socrates' name for the beliefs of the man in the street was 'bogies' to scare children.

24. The Spartans used to seat their guests out of the sun at all public spectacles, and themselves sat where they could.

25. Socrates gave as his reason for declining an invitation to the court of Perdiccas, 'I have no wish to go down to my grave with ignominy'; implying that he would accept no favour which he could not repay.

26. The scriptures of the Ephesians contain an exhortation to practise frequent remembrance of some bygone example of virtuous life.

27. The Pythagoreans enjoin contemplation of the heavens

1. Thus Marcus warns the philosopher not to exchange the quiet of his own soul for the perturbations of the world.

every morning, to remind themselves how changelessly and punctually those bodies perform their appointed task, and also to put them in mind of orderliness, purity and naked simplicity – for no veil clothes a star.

28. Think of Socrates, wrapped in the sheepskin after [1] Xantippe had walked off with his cloak, and what he said to his friends when they recoiled in embarrassment at seeing him so arrayed.

29. In reading and writing, you cannot lay down rules until you have learnt to obey them. Much more so in life.

30. 'Slavish by nature, reason is not for thee.' *

31. '. . . then laughed my heart within me.'†

32. 'Virtue they will but abuse, and taunt her with bitter reviling.'‡

33. 'The fool looks for figs in winter; so is he who looks for children when the season is past.'§

34. 'While you are kissing your child,' Epictetus once said, 'murmur under your breath, tomorrow it may be dead.' 'Ominous words,' they told him. 'Not at all,' said he, 'but

---

1. No record of this incident has been found. We know, however, that Socrates consistently refused to be provoked by Xantippe's asperities. According to Diogenes Laertius, he was once asked if he did not find her continual upbraidings intolerable. 'Do you find the cackling of your geese intolerable?' he said. 'No,' was the reply, 'for they provide me with eggs and young goslings.' 'And so does she provide me with children,' smiled Socrates. Marcus may be referring to some similar instance of the good-natured tolerance which he so frequently enjoins upon himself.

* Source unknown.   † Homer, *Odyssey*, iv. 413.
‡ Hesiod, *Works & Days*, 185 (adapted).   § Epictetus, iii, 24, 87.

only signifying an act of nature. Would it be ominous to speak of the gathering of ripe corn.'*

35. 'Green grape, ripe cluster, raisin; every step a change, not into what is not, but what is yet to be.'†

36. 'The robber of your free will,' writes Epictetus, 'does not exist.' ‡

37. He says, too, that we ought to evolve some proper system for our use of the assent. In regard to the impulses, we must take care to keep them always subject to modification, free from self-interest, and duly proportioned to the merits of the case. Desires also should be restrained to the utmost, and aversions confined to matters under our own control.

38. 'There is no triviality at issue here,' he says, 'but a plain question of sanity or insanity.'

39. 'Which is it your will to have?' Socrates would ask. 'Souls of reasonable or unreasonable men?' 'Reasonable.' 'Reasonable men who are sound, or sick?' 'Sound.' 'Then why not go seek for them?' 'Because we already have them.' 'In that case, then, why all your strife and contention?'

* Epictetus, 91.
† ibid., 92.
‡ ibid., iii, 22, 105.

BOOK TWELVE

1. All the blessings which you pray to obtain hereafter could be yours today, if you did not deny them to yourself. You have only to have done with the past altogether, commit the future to providence, and simply seek to direct the present hour aright into the paths of holiness and justice : holiness, by a loving acceptance of your apportioned lot, since Nature produced it for you and you for it : justice, in your speech by a frank and straightforward truthfulness, and in your acts by a respect for law and for every man's rights. Allow yourself, too, no hindrance from the malice, misconceptions or slanders of others, nor yet from any sensations this fleshy frame may feel; its afflicted part will look to itself. The hour for your departure draws near; if you will but forget all else and pay sole regard to the helmsman of your soul and the divine spark within you – if you will but exchange your fear of having to end your life some day for a fear of failing even to begin it on nature's true principles – you can yet become a man, worthy of the universe that gave you birth, instead of a stranger in your own homeland, bewildered by each day's happenings as though by wonders unlooked for, and ever hanging upon this one or the next.

2. God views the inner minds of men, stripped of every material sheath and husk and dross. Acting through his thought alone, he makes contact solely with that in them which is an outflow from himself. School yourself to do like-wise, and you will be spared many a distraction; for who that looks past this fleshly covering will ever harass himself with

visions of raiment, housing, reputation, or any of the rest of life's costume and scenery?

3. You are composed of three parts : body, breath, and mind. The first two merely belong to you in the sense that you are responsible for their care; the last alone is truly yours. If, then, you put away from this real self – from your understanding, that is – everything that others do or say and everything you yourself did or said in the past, together with every anxiety about the future, and everything affecting the body or its partner breath that is outside your own control, as well as everything that swirls about you in the eddy of outward circumstance, so that the powers of your mind, kept thus aloof and unspotted from all that destiny can do, may live their own life in independence, doing what is just, consenting to what befalls, and speaking what is true – if, I say, you put away from this master-faculty of yours every such clinging attachment, and whatever lies in the years ahead or the years behind, teaching yourself to become what Empedocles calls a 'totally rounded orb, in its own rotundity joying', and to be concerned solely with the life which you are now living, the life of the present moment, then until death comes you will be able to pass the rest of your days in freedom from all anxiety, and in kindliness and good favour with the deity within you.

4. I often marvel how it is that though each man loves himself beyond all else, he should yet value his own opinion of himself less than that of others. Assuredly if some god or sage counsellor were to stand beside him and bid him harbour no thought or purpose in his heart without straightway publishing it abroad, he could not endure it for so much as a single day. So much more regard have we for our neighbours' judgement of us than for our own.

5. Can the gods, who have contrived all else so well and so benevolently, have overlooked this one thing, that even eminently virtuous men, men in the closest correspondence with the divine and living in intimate union with it through their good works and devotion, should know no re-birth after their death, but be doomed to utter extinction? However, should this indeed be their lot, rest assured that if there had been need for some different plan, it would have been so ordained; had it accorded with Nature, Nature would have brought it to pass. Therefore, from its not being so (if in truth it is not), you may have all confidence that it ought not to be so. Surely you can see that in raising idle questions like this you are indicting the deity? For should we even be joining issue with the gods in this way, unless they were supremely good and just? And if they are, how could they ever have permitted anything to be unfairly or unreasonably neglected in their dispositions for the universe?

6. Practise, even when success looks hopeless. The left hand, inept in other respects for lack of practice, can grasp the reins more firmly than the right, because here it has had practice.

7. Meditate upon what you ought to be in body and soul when death overtakes you; meditate upon the brevity of life, and the measureless gulfs of eternity behind it and before, and upon the frailty of everything material.

8. Look at the inmost causes of things, stripped of their husks; note the intentions that underlie actions; study the essences of pain, pleasure, death, glory; observe how man's disquiet is all of his own making, and how troubles come never from another's hand, but like all else are creatures of our own opinion.

9. In the management of your principles, take example by the

pugilist, not the swordsman. One puts down his blade and has to pick it up again; the other is never without his hand, and so needs only to clench it.

10. See what things consist of; resolve them into their matter, form, and purpose.

11. How ample are the privileges vouchsafed to man – to do nothing but what God will approve, and accept everything God may assign!

12. No blame for the order of things can lie with the gods, since nothing amiss can be done by them, either willingly or otherwise; nor yet with men, whose misdoings are none of their own volition. Abstain then from all thoughts of blame.

13. How ludicrous and outlandish is astonishment at anything that happens in life!

14. There is a doom inexorable and a law inviolable, or there is a providence that can be merciful, or else there is a chaos that is purposeless and ungoverned. If a resistless fate, why try to struggle against it? If a providence willing to show mercy, do your best to deserve its divine succour. If a chaos undirected, give thanks that amid such stormy seas you have within you a mind at the helm. If the waters overwhelm you, let them overwhelm flesh, breath, and all else, but they will never make shipwreck of the mind.

15. Does the lantern's flame shine with undimmed brilliance until it is quenched, yet shall truth, wisdom, and justice die within you before you yourself are extinguished?

16. At the impression that somebody has done wrong, reflect, 'What certainty have I that it is wrong?' Furthermore, even if it is, may he not already have reproached himself for

it, fully as much as though his nails had visibly rent his features? To wish that a rogue would never do wrong is like wishing that fig-trees would never have any sour juice in their fruit, infants never cry, horses never neigh, or any other of life's inevitabilities never come to pass. How, pray, could he act otherwise, with the character he has? If you find it so vexatious, then reform it.

17. If it is not the right thing to do, never do it; if it is not the truth, never say it. Keep your impulses in hand.

18. Always look at the whole of a thing. Find what it is that makes its impression on you, then open it up and dissect it into cause, matter, purpose, and the length of time before it must end.

19. Try to see, before it is too late, that you have within you something higher and more godlike than mere instincts which move your emotions and twitch you like a puppet. Which of these is it, then, that is clouding my understanding at this moment? Fear, jealousy, lust, or some other?

20. Firstly, avoid all actions that are haphazard or purposeless; and secondly, let every action aim solely at the common good.

21. Soon enough, remember, you yourself must become a vagrant thing of nothingness; soon enough everything that now meets your eye, together with all those in whom is now the breath of life, must be no more. For all things are born to change and pass away and perish, that others in their turn may come to be.

22. Everything is but what your opinion makes it; and that opinion lies with yourself. Renounce it when you will, and at

once you have rounded the foreland and all is calm; a tranquil sea, a tideless haven.

23. When an operation, no matter of what sort, is brought to a close at the right moment, the stoppage does it no harm and the agent himself is no worse for discontinuing his action. So if life itself – which is nothing but the totality of all our operations – also ceases when the time comes, it takes no hurt by its mere cessation, nor is he adversely affected who thus brings the whole series of his operations to its timely conclusion. But the proper hour and term are fixed by nature: if not by a man's own nature – as, for example, through old age – then at all events by great Nature herself, by whose continuous renewing of her every part the universe remains forever young and vigorous. Whatever serves the purpose of the Whole is kept always fair and blooming. It follows, then, that the ending of his life can be no evil to a man – for, being a thing outside his control and innocent of all self-seeking, there is nothing in it to degrade him – nay, it is even a good, inasmuch as for the universe it is something opportune, serviceable and in keeping with all else. Thus, by following the way of God and being at one with him in thought, man is borne onward by the divine hand.

24. There are three counsels worth keeping in mind. The first concerns actions: these should never be undertaken at random, nor in ways unsanctioned by justice. You must remember that all outward events are the result of either chance or providence; and you cannot reprimand chance or impeach providence. In the second place, think well what everything is, from earliest seed to birth of soul and from soul's birth to its ultimate surrender; what the thing is compounded of, and what it will dissolve into. Thirdly, imagine yourself suddenly carried up into the clouds and looking down on the whole

panorama of human activities: how the scene would excite your contempt, now that you could discern the multitude of aerial and heavenly beings who throng around them. Furthermore, reflect that no matter how often upborne in this way, you would still behold the same sights, in all their monotony and transience. Yet these are the things of which we make such a boast!

25. Once dismiss the view you take, and you are out of danger. Who, then, is hindering such dismissal?

26. When you let yourself feel resentment at a thing, you forget that nothing can come about except in obedience to Nature; that any misconduct in the matter was none of yours; and moreover, that this is the only way in which things have always happened, will always happen, and do always happen. You are forgetting, too, the closeness of man's brotherhood with his kind; a brotherhood not of blood or human seed, but of a common intelligence; and that this intelligence in every man is God, an emanation from the deity. You forget that nothing is properly a man's own, for even his child, his body, his soul itself, all come from this same God; also, that all things depend upon opinion; also, that the passing moment is all that a man can ever live or lose.

27. Ponder the lives of the men who have set no bounds to their passions, the men who have reached the very summits of glory, disaster, odium, or any other of the peaks of chance; and then consider, 'Where are they all now?' Vapour, ashes, a tale; perhaps not even a tale. Contemplate the numerous examples: Fabius Catullinus on his estate, Lucius Lupus in his gardens, Stertinius at Baiae, Tiberius at Capri, Velius Rufus; any instance at all of what pride can set its heart upon. How ignoble are all their strivings! How much more

befitting a philosopher it were to aim at justice, temperance and fealty to the gods – yet always with simplicity, for the pride that swells beneath a garb of humility is of all things the most intolerable.

28. To those who insist, 'Where have you ever seen the gods, and how can you be so assured of their existence, that you worship them in this way?' my answer is, 'For one thing, they are perfectly visible to the eye.[1] For another, I have never seen my own soul either, but none the less do I venerate that. So it is with the gods; it is experience which proves their power every day, and therefore I am satisfied that they exist, and I do them reverence.'

29. For a life that is sound and secure, cultivate a thorough insight into things and discover their essence, matter, and cause; put your whole heart into doing what is just, and speaking what is true; and for the rest, know the joy of life by piling good deed on good deed until no rift or cranny appears between them.

30. Sunlight is all one, even when it is broken up by walls, mountains, and a host of other things. Substance is all one, even when it is parcelled out among the numberless living bodies of different sorts, each with its own special qualities. Soul is all one, even when it is distributed among countless natures of every kind in countless differing proportions. Even soul that is gifted with the additional quality of thought, though apparently divisible, is likewise all one. For the other parts of all those organisms – their breath, for example – are material things, incapable of sensation, which have no affinity with each other and are only kept together by the unifying

1. The Stoics believed the stars to be divine.

pressure of gravitation. But thought, by its very nature, tends spontaneously towards anything of its own kind and mingles with it; so that the instinct for unity is not frustrated.

31. Why do you hunger for length of days? Is it to experience sensations and desires, or increase or cessation of growth? Is it to make use of the powers of speech or thought? Does any of these things seem really worth coveting? Then if you think them beneath your notice, press on towards the final goal of all – which is the following of reason and of God. But to prize this, you must remember, is incompatible with any feelings of resentment that death will rob you of the others.

32. How small a fraction of all the measureless infinity of time is allotted to each one of us; an instant, and it vanishes into eternity. How puny, too, is your portion of all the world's substance; how insignificant your share of all the world's soul; on how minute a speck of the whole earth do you creep. As you ponder these things, make up your mind that nothing is of any import save to do what your own nature directs, and to bear what the world's Nature sends you.

33. How is my soul's helmsman going about his task? For in that lies everything. All else, within my control or beyond it, is dead bones and vapour.

34. Nothing will more encourage a contempt for death than the reflection that even men who accounted pleasure a good and pain an evil have nevertheless been able to despise it.

35. When a man finds his sole good in that which the appointed hour brings him; when he cares not if his actions be many or few, so they accord with strict reason; when it matters nought to him whether his glimpse of this world be long or fleeting – not death itself can be a thing of terror for him.

36. O man, citizenship of this great world-city has been yours. Whether for five years or fivescore, what is that to you? Whatever the law of that city decrees is fair to one and all alike. Wherein, then, is your grievance? You are not ejected from the city by any unjust judge or tyrant, but by the selfsame Nature which brought you into it; just as when an actor is dismissed by the manager who engaged him. 'But I have played no more than three of the five acts.' Just so; in your drama of life, three acts are all the play. Its point of completeness is determined by him who formerly sanctioned your creation, and today sanctions your dissolution. Neither of those decisions lay within yourself. Pass on your way, then, with a smiling face, under the smile of him who bids you go.

MORE ABOUT PENGUINS, PELICANS
AND PUFFINS

For further information about books available from Penguins please write to
Dept EP, Penguin Books Ltd, Harmondsworth, Middlesex UB7 ODA.

In the U.S.A.: For a complete list of books available from Penguins in the
United States write to Dept DG, Penguin Books, 299 Murray Hill Parkway,
East Rutherford, New Jersey 07073.

In Canada: For a complete list of books available from Penguins in Canada
write to Penguin Books Canada Ltd, 2801 John Street, Markham, Ontario
L3R 1B4.

In Australia: For a complete list of books available from Penguins in Australia
write to the Marketing Department, Penguin Books Australia Ltd, P.O.
Box 257, Ringwood, Victoria 3134.

In New Zealand: For a complete list of books available from Penguins in New
Zealand write to the Marketing Department, Penguin Books (N.Z.) Ltd,
P.O. Box 4019, Auckland 10.

In India: For a complete list of books available from Penguins in India write
to Penguin Overseas Ltd, 706 Eros Apartments, 56 Nehru Place, New Delhi
110019.

THE PENGUIN CLASSICS

EARLY CHRISTIAN WRITINGS
THE APOSTOLIC FATHERS

Translated by Maxwell Staniforth

These writings, translated from the Greek, are the earliest and most venerable examples of the mass of ecclesiastical literature produced in the first centuries A.D. They are the work of a group known as the Apostolic Fathers, who faithfully preserved the apostolic teaching and tradition between the time of the apostles and the late second century.

THOMAS À KEMPIS
THE IMITATION OF CHRIST

Translated by Leo Sherley-Price

Thomas à Kempis (1380–1471) had a wide knowledge of the Scriptures and classical philosophy, and although most of his life was spent in a Dutch monastery, he possessed a deep understanding of human nature. The book has exercised a profound influence for over 500 years and after the Bible is probably the best-known and loved book in the Christian world.

BEDE
A HISTORY OF THE ENGLISH CHURCH AND PEOPLE

Translated by Leo Sherley-Price

This wonderfully alive tapestry of Saxon England and Celtic Britain written in A.D. 731 still has the power to transport us back to these crucially formative years when Britain had still to be wrought into one entity. Leo Sherley-Price has produced an accurate and readable version of Bede's work in modern English.

PENGUIN CLASSICS

'Penguin continue to pour out the jewels of the world's classics in translation . . . There are now nearly enough to keep a man happy on a desert island until the boat comes in' – Philip Howard in *The Times*

A selection

ALEXANDER DUMAS
THE THREE MUSKETEERS

Translated by Lord Sudley

CAO XUEQUIN AND GAO E
THE STORY OF THE STONE

(also known as *The Dream of the Red Chamber*)

VOLUME 4: THE DEBT OF TEARS

Translated by John Minford

ANTON CHEKHOV
THE KISS AND OTHER STORIES

Translated by Ronald Wilks

ALEXANDER PUSHKIN
THE BRONZE HORSEMAN

Translated by D. M. Thomas

OVID
THE EROTIC POEMS

Translated by Peter Greene

MADAME DE SÉVIGNÉ
SELECTED LETTERS

Translated by Leonard Tancock